THE BIG BOOK OF
Latvian Mittens

100 knitting patterns for
colourful Latvian mittens

Ieva Ozolina

DAVID & CHARLES

www.davidandcharles.com

Contents

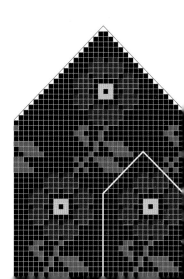

Introduction

Mittens play an important role in Latvia's culture and history. For several centuries they were the most common type of gift in the country, and are thought by some to have magical qualities.

Mittens were most often given as wedding gifts and the act of making them for special occasions still continues today. Traditionally, every bride-to-be was expected to fill a "hope chest", and the most lavish chests contained several hundred pairs of handmade mittens. Mittens were also given to the family of the couple and anyone involved in organising the wedding. Nowadays, Latvian mittens, with their distinctive shape and diverse range of colours and patterns, are still a winter essential.

Most of the patterns are derived from Latvian mythology and incorporate various folk symbols. Each knitted design has a different meaning and therefore every mitten has its own special story. Choose your favourites from this collection of 100 stylish patterns, and learn how to create your own beautiful mittens, along with gloves, fingerless mittens, fingerless gloves and wrist warmers.

I have been looking for samples of authentic gloves and mittens all over Latvia and have had help from the Cēsis History and Art Museum and the Liepaja Museum, who both kindly agreed to share their carefully preserved historical collections with me.

Tools and materials

YARN

A natural 2-ply 100% wool is recommended as the best yarn to use and is also the yarn that has been traditionally used for Latvian mittens. Depending on your tension (gauge) (see Before you begin), you may be able to use 4-ply sock weight yarn of approximately 400m (437yd) per 100g (3½oz).

NEEDLES

For mitten and glove knitting, five double-pointed metal needles are recommended in sizes 1.5mm-2.0mm (US sizes 000-0) and length 20cm (8in), depending on your tension (gauge) (see Before you begin). Wooden or bamboo needles are not recommended because the small sizes are too fragile and can snap easily. The magic loop technique is not recommended either, because these patterns are specifically designed for knitting with five double-pointed needles and would therefore be almost impossible to follow using the magic loop technique.

OTHER USEFUL EQUIPMENT

- A pair of sharp scissors – for snipping yarn.

- A hard, see-through ruler – for measuring tension (gauge).

- A tape measure – for measuring the length of longer pieces of knitting.

- A tapestry/wool needle – blunt ended (a pointy needle will split your yarn and spoil your knitting).

- Safety pins – for separating stitches for glove fingers.

- Rust-proof pins with glass heads (for visibility) – for measuring your tension squares and blocking your work.

- A blocking board or mitten/glove blockers for blocking your work.

- Stitch markers – to mark the start of the round, or to mark a pattern repeat.

- Row counter – helpful to keep a note of how many rows you've knitted.

- Notebook and pen – as an alternative to a row counter, or to make notes of your tension or any alterations or adaptations you make to a pattern.

- Project bag – perfect for keeping your work and equipment in.

Before you begin

CALCULATING YARN REQUIREMENTS

Follow the project chart as a guide for using colours – each coloured square on the chart represents the colour of the yarn used for a stitch. The main base colour is the background colour.

For each pair of mittens, fingerless mittens or fingerless gloves, you will need: approximately 50g (175m/192yd) of the base colour, plus 25g (87.5m/96yd) for each contrast colour.

For each pair of gloves, you will need: approximately 50g (175m/192yd) of the base colour, plus 25g (87.5m/96yd) for each contrast colour.

For each pair of wrist warmers, you will need: approximately 25g (87.5m/96yd) of the base colour, plus 10g (35m/39yd) for each contrast colour.

These amounts are intended as a general guide and include extra grams than required, so that you won't run out of yarn. Finished mittens usually weigh 50-100g (1¾-3½oz), gloves 75-100g (2½-3½oz), fingerless gloves and fingerless mittens 50-70g (1¾-2½oz) and wrist warmers 20-30g (¾-1oz). Note, for some projects, not all of the contrast colour will be used. If you work to a different tension or substitute cuff options or make your project longer, you may require more yarn than stated.

MEASURING TENSION (GAUGE)

For regular size mittens, knit with 1.5mm (US size 000) needles to a tension (gauge) of 17 stitches and 22 rows to measure 5 x 5cm (2 x 2in).

For regular size gloves, knit with 2mm (US size 0) needles to a tension (gauge) of 17 stitches and 20 rows to measure 5 x 5cm (2 x 2in).

If you knit very tight or want to make a larger mitten or glove, use needles up to size 2.5mm (US size 1-2). Try the mitten or glove on while you are working to make sure it fits as you prefer.

Adjust your needles larger or smaller to achieve the correct tension and knitted fabric. Note that if you are using two or more colours, the fabric tends to shrink due to the tension of the back strands.

READING CHARTS

- Each square on the chart represents one stitch. Knit each stitch in the colour shown on the chart.

- Read all charts from right to left. Where one chart is provided for the hand, repeat the chart twice. Where two charts are provided for the front and back of the hand, follow the right chart first, then follow the left chart.

- Where a thumb chart is provided separately, follow this for the thumb pattern. Where the thumb pattern is outlined on the main mitten chart, follow the thumb section outlined, making sure to work it on the correct needle as instructed in Step 4 of the Basic mitten recipe.

- For full details on the cuff method used, see Cuff options.

- The sloping sections of the mitten and thumb charts represent the decreases.

- Where the chart reduces in width by one square, this indicates a decrease of one stitch for each pattern repeat (use k2tog or skpo); for two squares use a left- or right-slanting double decrease to reduce two stitches for each pattern repeat (see Symbols and abbreviations).

- Where the chart increases in width by one square, this indicates an increase of one stitch for each pattern repeat. Use an M1 increase (see Symbols and abbreviations).

STRANDING YARN

When you are working with one or more strands of yarn at a time, it is important to keep the balls of yarn separated so that they do not become tangled. It helps if you can place one ball of yarn on your right and one ball of yarn on your left.

Always carry the yarn not being used loosely across the back of your work until you need it next, and don't pull it too tightly, otherwise your knitting will pucker.

When changing colour, always choose one colour that will feed in to your knitting above the other colour (from the top) and feed the other colour in from the bottom. If you maintain this order throughout your knitting, your patterning will look uniform and neat.

BLOCKING YOUR PROJECTS

Once you have finished your mittens, gloves or wrist warmers, it is recommended to block them, to even out the stitches. Spray one side of knitting with cold water until wet, but not saturated. Gently press the water into the stitches with your hands, then pin flat to dry. Repeat for the opposite side. If you feel that your project needs stretching slightly to fit, pin to the size desired (or use a mitten or glove blocker) and leave to dry.

Symbols and abbreviations

This handy guide explains the symbols and abbreviations used in this book:

INSTRUCTIONS	CHART SYMBOL
K (knit) – Insert the right needle into the front of the next stitch on left needle, wrap the yarn around the right needle from back to front and pull the needle through the stitch to the front of work to create a loop on right needle. Take the original stitch off the tip of the left needle, leaving the new knit stitch on the right needle.	▢ ▯
P (purl) – Insert the right needle into the next stitch on the left needle from the back of the stitch to the front, wrap the yarn around the right needle anti-clockwise and pull the needle through the stitch to the back of work to create a loop on right needle. Take the original stitch off the tip of the left needle, leaving the new purl stitch on the right needle.	⊟
K2tog (knit 2 stitches together) – Insert the right needle into the next 2 stitches on left needle and knit them together as one stitch. (A diagonal line in a square may also indicate an embroidery stitch - see Embroidery stitch symbol).	◹
Skpo (slip, knit, pass over) – Insert the right needle into the next stitch knitwise and slip the stitch to the right needle, without knitting it. Knit the next stitch. Insert the left needle into the slipped stitch on the right needle. Lift the slipped stitch and pass it over the knitted stitch and off the needle. (A diagonal line in a square may also indicate an embroidery stitch - see Embroidery stitch symbol).	◺
CDD (centred double decrease) – Insert the right needle into the next 2 stitches together knitwise and slip them to the right needle, without knitting them. Knit the next stitch. Insert the left needle into the slipped stitches on the right needle. Lift the slipped stitches together and pass them over the knit stitch and off the needle. This creates a centred decrease of 2 stitches. Note: When using stitch markers to mark the position of these decreases, place them between the 2nd and 3rd stitch. When working the decrease, remove the marker after slipping the first 2 stitches, then replace it after completing the decrease. This ensures that a column of centred decreases will line up.	△
Slipped stitch – Slip the stitch from the left needle to the right needle, as if to purl, without knitting it. This can be used to create a two-coloured pattern when the previous row (and therefore any slipped stitch) is a different colour.	⩘

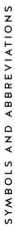

3-into-3 – Insert the right needle into back of next 3 stitches and knit them together without dropping them off the left needle. Wrap the yarn around the right needle, then knit into the back of the same 3 stitches again, this time dropping them off the left needle.	⊠3⊠
C4B (cable back over 4 stitches) – Slip next 2 stitches onto a cable needle, hold at back of work, knit next 2 stitches then knit 2 stitches from cable needle (for a right slanting cable).	
YO (yarn over) – Wrap the yarn over the needle to add an extra stitch.	○
Latvian Braid – See Cuff options for full instructions	
Embroidery stitch – Where indicated, once knitting is complete, work embroidery stitches around using colour indicated in the instructions.	

See Cuff options for additional symbols used in the charts.

Double right-slanting decrease (k3tog) – Insert the right needle into the next 3 stitches on left needle and knit them together as one stitch. This creates a decrease of 2 stitches, slanting to the right.

Double left-slanting decrease (sk2po) – Insert the right needle into the next stitch knitwise and slip the stitch to the right needle, without knitting it. Knit the next 2 stitches together as one stitch. Insert the left needle into the slipped stitch on the right needle. Lift the slipped stitch and pass it over the k2tog stitches and off the needle. This creates a decrease of 2 stitches, slanting to the left.

M1 (make 1 stitch) – Insert the left needle under the bar between stitches from front to back and lift it to create a loop. Knit into the back of this loop.

Stocking stitch (stockinette) – Work stocking stitch in the round by knitting every round. Work stocking stitch flat by alternating between knit rows and purl rows.

Garter stitch – Work garter stitch in the round by alternating between knit rounds and purl rounds. Work garter stitch flat by knitting every row.

Basic mitten recipe

GETTING STARTED

All of the mittens in this book follow the same basic knitting pattern, which consists of a cuff, stem, palm, thumb and a cast off (bind off) shaping section.

Follow the instructions below alongside the colour chart of your chosen design, to create your Latvian mittens.

The charts use symbols which are explained in the Symbols and abbreviations section. It is important to first familiarise yourself with the symbols used.

Remember to check your tension (gauge) before knitting a full mitten (see Before you begin).

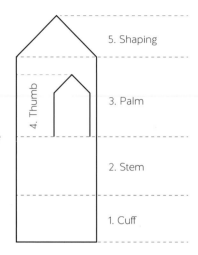

5. Shaping

4. Thumb

3. Palm

2. Stem

1. Cuff

STEP 1 – CAST ON

1. Using any cast-on method, cast on the total amount of the stitches onto one needle (Figure A). The total amount of stitches required is specified in each pattern.

2. Divide the stitches equally over 4 double-pointed needles when working the first round of the cuff (Figure B).

3. Tie the cast-on tail end with the working yarn, so that there is no gap between the stitches on the first and last needles.

4. Use one of the yarn tails as a marker, to mark the start of the round, and move it up every few rounds.

5. Always knit from right to left.

STEP 2 – THE CUFF

Start the cuff according to the pattern in the chart. See Cuff options for instructions for "Simple Cuff", "The Notches", "The Fringe" and "Latvian Braid".

You can customise your cuff by making it longer or shorter than specified. You can substitute any of the cuffs if you prefer a different one than shown in the chart. A simple cuff in the base colour or a contrast colour can work well with any mitten.

STEP 3 – THE BODY

The rest of the mitten is completed by following the pattern shown in the chart, reading the chart(s) from right to left on every round. If no textured or special stitches are used, change colours as shown in the chart and work in stocking (stockinette) stitch (knitting every round).

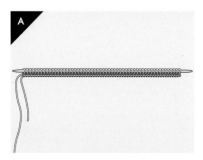

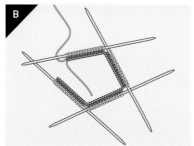

STEP 4 – MARK THE THUMB

1. The thumb is worked over the total amount of stitches specified in each pattern.

2. The thumb is created on Needle 3 for the right hand and Needle 2 for the left hand.

3. Mark the location of the thumb with a contrast colour yarn as follows: knit the stitches for the thumb with scrap yarn (choose a strong yarn of a similar weight or thinner) (Figure C).

Tie the loose ends of the scrap yarn together so that it does not pull out accidentally (Figure D).

4. Slide these thumb stitches back onto the left needle, and work them again with working yarn, according to your pattern (Figure E).

STEP 5 – FINISH THE BODY

To finish the body, continue according to the pattern, reading the chart(s) from right to left on every round, until the first decrease round is reached.

STEP 6 – DECREASE

The decrease of a Latvian mitten is made in the form of a triangle.

1. One decrease round reduces 4 stitches in total.

2. You will decrease at the beginning and at the end of alternate needles: at the beginning of Needle 1 and Needle 3; at the end of Needle 2 and Needle 4. This makes it easier to keep track of your decreases.

3. At the beginning of Needle 1 and Needle 3: knit 1, skpo (see Symbols and abbreviations), knit the remaining stitches.

4. At the ends of Needle 2 and Needle 4: knit to the last 3 stitches, k2tog (see Symbols and abbreviations), knit 1.

5. Continue decreasing in this way until you have only 2 stitches left on each needle.

6. Using tapestry/wool needle, take the thread through the stitches and pull the yarn tail through to the wrong side and secure (Figure F).

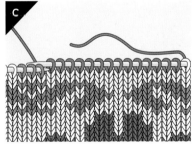

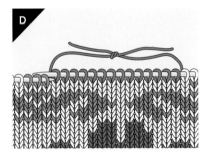

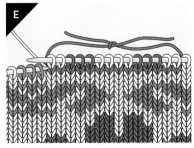

STEP 7 – THE THUMB

1. Use one needle to pick up the stitches directly above the scrap yarn – picking up the right leg of each stitch and working from right to left. Use a second needle to pick up the stitches directly below the scrap yarn in exactly the same way (Figure G).

2. Pick up 1 stitch at each opposite "corner" of the thumbhole between the lower and upper needles (Figure H). Use lifted strand stitch by inserting the left needle under the loop of yarn, from the back, and slipping it onto the right needle.

3. Rearrange the stitches so that they are evenly distributed on four needles. If the stitch count is not divisible by 4, make sure that the extra 2 stitches picked up at the corners are on Needles 1 and 3, or on Needles 2 and 4 (Figure I).

4. Rejoin the main colour yarn – join it to the stitch that sits to the right of the first stitch.

5. Remove the scrap yarn used to mark the thumb.

6. In the first round, twist the picked up corner stitches when knitting them to avoid making holes, by inserting the right needle purlwise into the front of the corner stitch, then manoeuvre the right needle over the tip of the left needle (don't let the stitch fall off) so that it sits behind the left needle (needles are now in the usual position for knit stitch).

7. Knit straight following the chart, until the thumb measures the required length or until the base of your thumbnail is reached. Note the following for the thumb knitting:

- In most mittens, the thumb chart is outlined on the main mitten chart. These thumbs blend seamlessly into the mitten.

- For others, the thumb chart pattern is a contrast pattern and will appear as a separate chart.

- The additional corner stitches picked up for the thumb are not included in the chart for any thumb pattern. For these stitches you knit them in background colour – hence you treat the thumb front and thumb back as two separate patterns, separated by a column of background stitches.

STEP 8 – THUMB DECREASE

1. Thumb decreases are worked in the same way as mitten decreases – working a decrease at the beginning and at the end of alternate needles.

2. At the beginning of a needle decrease (Needles 1 and 3): knit 1, skpo (see Symbols and abbreviations).

3. At the end of a needle decrease (Needles 2 and 4): k2tog, knit 1.

4. Continue decreasing until there are 10 stitches in total – 5 stitches left on front side needles and 5 stitches left on back side needles (10 stitches over four needles).

5. Divide all stitches between two needles – 5 stitches on one needle and 5 on another – and continue knitting with the third needle.

6. Knit the last round as follows: *sk2po (see Symbols and abbreviations), k2tog; repeat from * once more (see Symbols and abbreviations).

7. Cut the yarn and pull through the stitches. Turn the thumb inside out, pull the yarn tail through to the wrong side and secure. If there are holes at the base of the thumb, use the yarn tail there to tighten them up.

STEP 9 – FINISH

Sew in any remaining ends and block your mittens (see Before you begin).

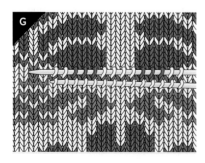

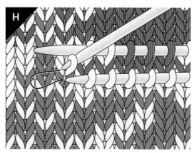

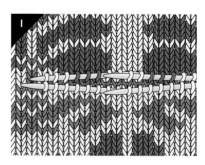

Basic glove recipe

GETTING STARTED

All of the gloves in this book follow the same basic knitting pattern, which consists of a cuff, body, fingers and thumb.

Follow the instructions below, alongside the colour chart of your chosen design, to create your Latvian gloves.

The charts use symbols which are fully explained in the Symbols and abbreviations section. It is important to first familiarise yourself with the symbols used.

Remember to check your tension (gauge) before knitting a full mitten (see Before you begin).

STEPS 1 AND 2 – CAST ON AND THE CUFF

Begin by follows Steps 1 and 2 for the Basic mitten recipe to cast on and work the cuff.

STEP 3 – THE BODY

The rest of the glove is completed by following the pattern shown in the chart, reading the chart(s) from right to left on every round. If no textured or special stitches are used, change colours as shown in the chart and work in stocking (stockinette) stitch (knitting every round).

STEP 4 – MARK THE THUMB

Work as for Step 4 of the Basic mitten recipe to mark the thumb using scrap yarn.

STEP 5 – FINISH THE BODY

To finish the body, continue according to the pattern, reading the chart(s) from right to left on every round, until the start of your little finger.

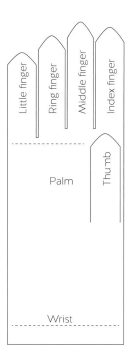

Note that "Front" refers to the part of the glove that covers the back of the hand and "Back" refers to the part of the glove that covers the palm.

STEP 6 – KNIT THE FINGERS

The stitches you have now will be divided among the four fingers (with extra stitches cast on between each finger) (Figure A). Note that in some cases the tension (gauge) means that the gloves are worked with fewer than 72 stitches. Follow the chart(s) for the number of stitches to divide for each finger if different than these instructions.

1. Knit the fingers in the following order: the index finger, the middle finger, the ring finger and finally the little finger.

2. First, separate the little finger stitches into two sections (front and back) of 9 stitches each (18 stitches in total). Knit 1 row with scrap yarn, then transfer both sets of 9 stitches to safety pins for later (Figure B).

3. Before you start knitting the fingers, cast on an additional 3 stitches (Figure C) between the little finger (on the safety pins) and the other fingers (57 stitches in total) and knit 2 rounds. These rounds are necessary because other fingers start slightly higher than the little finger.

4. Then, using more safety pins, section off the stitches for the ring finger (3 next to little finger plus 2 x 8 stitches) and the middle finger (2 x 9 stitches).

5. You will have 20 stitches (2 x 10) remaining on the needles. These will be used for the index finger (Figure D).

6. Cast on 3 stitches between the index and middle fingers (Figure E) and divide your 23 stitches over 3 needles (8 + 8 + 7).

Knit in the round until the index finger measures the desired length or until it reaches halfway up your fingernail (Figure F).

7. You will now decrease the index finger. Knit to the last 2 stitches on Needle 1. Work these 2 together as follows: slip the second stitch over the first one, then knit this first stitch (Figure G).

8. Work this decrease over the last 2 stitches on each knitting needle, in each round, until there are 2 stitches left on each needle (6 stitches in total) (Figure H).

9. For each set of 2 stitches, slip the second stitch over the first one, but without knitting any stitches. There is 1 stitch remaining on each of your 3 needles (Figure I).

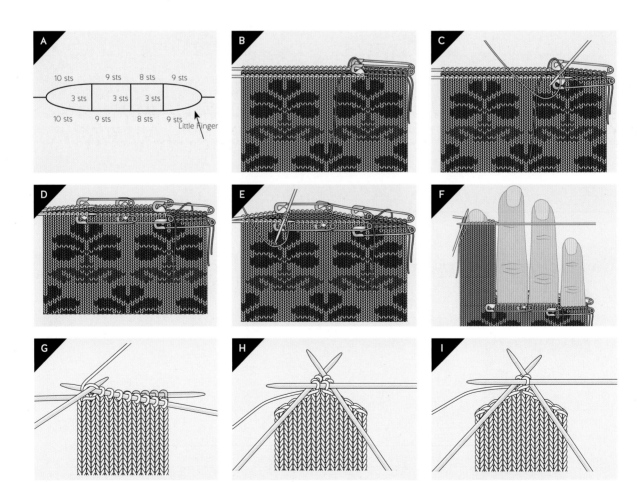

10. Cut the working yarn, leaving a tail about 15-20cm (6-8in) long. Using your tapestry/wool needle, thread this tail through the 3 remaining stitches (Figure J), and pull tight to fasten them together. Don't sew the end in yet.

11. You will now work the middle finger. You need to cast on 3 stitches between the middle finger and the ring finger, transfer one set of 9 stitches from the safety pin to your needles then pick up and knit 3 stitches from the base of the index finger (you can use a crochet hook to make picking up these stitches easier) (Figure K).

Finally, transfer the second set of 9 stitches to your needles. You now have 24 stitches, which you can divide into 8 stitches on each needle (Figure L). Now work as for the index finger, until you have fastened off.

12. Next, work the ring finger.

You will have a total of 19 stitches on hold, and will need to pick up 3 stitches from the base of the middle finger.

Divide your 22 stitches over 3 needles (8 + 7 + 7) (Figure M). Work the ring finger as for the index finger.

13. Now return to the little finger. Remove one of the safety pins (Figure N), carefully pull out the scrap yarn and place the 9 stitches on a needle (Figure O).

Repeat this process with the other 9 stitches (Figure P).

Finally, pick up and knit 3 stitches from the base of the ring finger (Figure Q).

Divide your 21 stitches over 3 needles: 7 stitches on each needle.

Work the little finger in the same way as the other fingers.

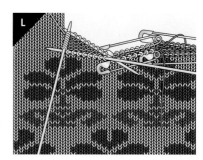

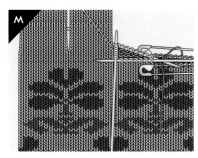

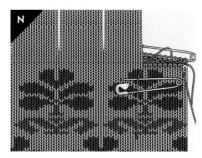

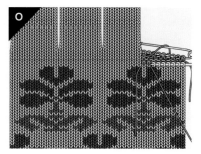

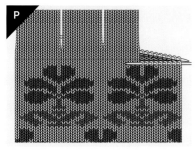

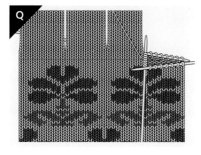

STEPS 7 AND 8 – THE THUMB AND THUMB DECREASES

Work the thumb according to Steps 7 and 8 for the Basic mitten recipe.

Note: For most gloves, the thumb is knitted in the base colour, but a few have separate charts.

STEP 9 – FINISH

1. Your gloves are almost ready (Figures R & S). Before you start weaving in the ends, make sure the gloves are the correct size and you are happy with them.

2. Now sew in the tails at the end of the decreases. Thread the tail onto your tapestry/wool needle, then insert the needle right in the middle of the fingertip and pull it down and through to the inside of the glove (Figure T).

3. When all the yarn tails are inside the glove (Figure U), turn it inside out (Figure V).

4. Thread a yarn tail onto your tapestry/wool needle and pass it through the finger decrease line (Figure W).

5. Then turn the needle in the opposite direction, towards the fingertip, and thread the needle through the stitches again (Figure X).

6. Trim and secure the thread, then repeat for all the finger/thumb tips (Figure Y). Sew in any other ends, using the tails to close up any holes at the base of the fingers.

7. Turn the glove right-side out (Figure Z).

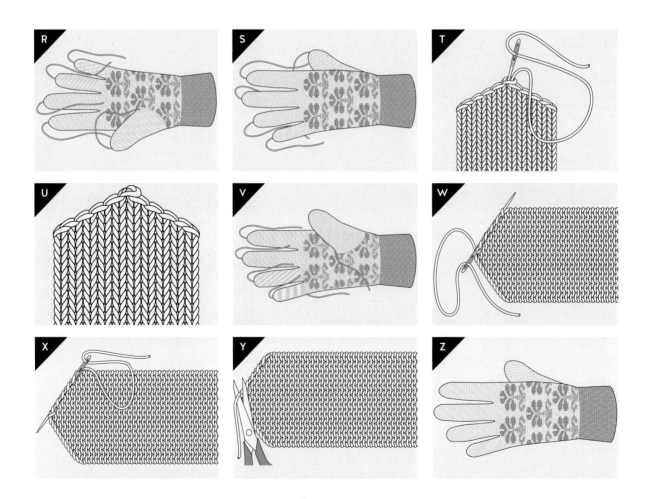

Fingerless recipes

FINGERLESS MITTENS

To make fingerless mittens (open top mittens with open tip thumb), follow Steps 1 to 5 from the Basic mitten recipe, ending the body where shown in the chart or until you have reached the upper joint of the little finger.

On the final round, cast off (bind off) all stitches (see Casting off).

Work Step 7 – The Thumb from the Basic mitten recipe, then cast off (bind off) and finish the thumb in the same way as for the hand section. If there are holes at the base of the thumb, use the yarn tail there to tighten them up.

To finish, sew in any other ends and block your fingerless mittens (see Before you begin).

FINGERLESS GLOVES

To make fingerless gloves (open tip fingered gloves), follow Steps 1 to 6 from the Basic glove recipe.

Once you divide the stitches, work each finger to the required length and cast off (bind off) each finger's stitches (see Casting off).

Work Step 7 – The Thumb from the Basic glove recipe, then cast off (bind off) and finish the thumb in the same way as for the fingers.

Make sure you are happy with the fingerless gloves before weaving in the ends as follows:

- Thread each tail onto your tapestry/wool needle, then pull it through to the inside of the glove. When all the yarn tails are inside the glove, turn it inside out.
- Sew the tails securely, working along the fabric in different directions and use the tails to close up any holes at the base of the fingers or thumb.
- Then turn the fingerless glove right-side out.

WRIST WARMERS

To make wrist warmers (cuffs of various length without coverage on the hand or fingers), work Steps 1 to 3 from the Basic mitten recipe, working to your preferred length. Wrist warmers can work the same cuff at both ends or work a different cuff at the bottom and top (see Cuff options).

To finish the wrist warmers on the last round, cast off (bind off) all stitches (see Casting off). Sew in any ends and block to your preferred measurements (see Before you begin).

CASTING OFF

When casting off all stitches, work as follows:

- Use the free needle to cast off the stitches on the first needle until one stitch remains.
- Drop the free needle and use the needle with the one remaining stitch to cast off the stitches on the next needle to the last stitch.
- Continue in this way to the last stitch on the last needle and fasten off this stitch. Use the yarn tail to close up the gap between the first and last stitches.

Cuff options

SIMPLE CUFF

The Simple cuff is represented on a chart as shown in Figure A.

1. Work 1 round in purl stitch.

2. Work 1 round in knit stitch.

3. Repeat these 2 rounds another 3 times, or as many times as indicated on the chart (the purl stitch round is represented by a dashed line on the chart; see Symbols and abbreviations).

THE FRINGE

The Fringe cuff is represented on a chart as shown in Figure B.

1. Work the first row in purl stitch and divide your stitches equally between 4 needles.

2. Hold your index finger behind the needles and wind the yarn 3 times, loosely, around the index finger from front to back. The wrong side of the knitting is facing you.

3. Insert the right needle into the next stitch on the left needle, knitwise, then insert the right needle under the wrapped yarn around the finger, purlwise (Figure C).

4. Pull the wrapped yarn through the stitch on the left needle and very carefully remove your finger. You now have the 3 loops of yarn on your right needle (Figure D). Take care not to pull the working yarn, otherwise you will pull out the loops just made. The loops will sit behind the needles, and note that the side of knitting facing you is the wrong side. Try to keep your loops the same size for every stitch.

5. Work in alternate colours, if desired (Figure E).

6. When all of the fringe is knitted, turn the knitting to the right side.

7. Knit 1 round in knit stitch, then follow the pattern chart. You can gently pull down on each loop after the knit round (Figure F).

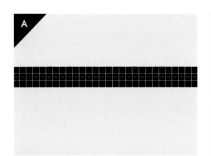

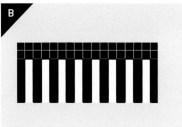

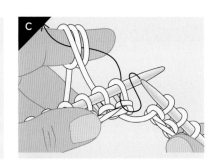

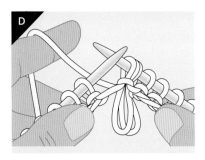

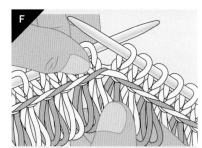

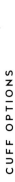

THE NOTCHES

The Notches cuff is represented on a chart as shown in Figure G.

The Notches is always worked over an odd number of rounds. The same number of rounds is worked in knit stitch before (Step 1) and after (Step 3) the folding round (Step 2). For example if the pattern says The Notches is worked over 11 rounds, work 5 rounds in knit stitch then work the folding round, then work 5 further rounds in knit (5 + 1 + 5 = 11 rounds).

1. Work 5 rounds (or as many rounds as shown in the chart before the folding round) in knit stitch.

2. Folding round: Knit 1 round as [K2tog, YO] to the end (see Symbols and abbreviations). Note that the yarn over creates a hole in your knitting. This round is the foldline.

3. Work a further 5 rounds (or the same number of rounds as worked in Step 1) in knit stitch.

4. Fold your knitting at the foldline, bringing the cast-on edge up at the back of your needles to meet the working edge.

5. For the next round, knit together one stitch from the left needle with one stitch from the cast-on edge of the knitting, making sure that these stitches are in line with each other. To do this, insert the right needle into the corresponding stitch along the cast-on edge (Figure H). Place this stitch on the tip of the left needle. Knit this stitch and the next stitch together as one stitch (Figure I). Repeat this process for the remainder of the round, to complete The Notches cuff.

LATVIAN BRAID

The Latvian Braid cuff is represented on a chart as shown in Figure J.

Knitted using two colours, over two rounds.

1. Choose one colour for A and another for B.

2. Knit the first round as follows: *k1 with A, k1 with B; repeat from * to the end of the round.

3. Bring both yarns forward between needles to the front of the work (Figure K).

4. Purl the second round in the same colour sequence: *p1 with A, p1 with B; repeat from * to the end of the round each time bringing the next colour over the yarn you have just knitted with, to create the braiding effect (Figure L).

5. Take both yarns between the needles to the back of work. Knit one row in the base colour of the pattern and then continue to follow the chart pattern.

6. To create a double Latvian Braid, repeat Step 4 once more, but each time passing the new yarn **under** the yarn you have just knitted with.

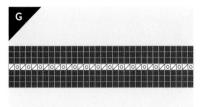

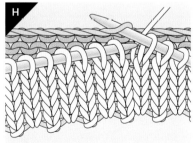

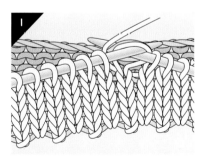

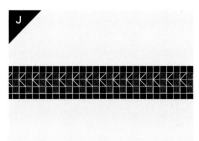

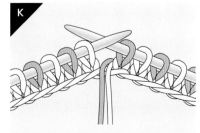

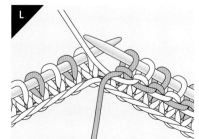

WINDFARM
MITTENS

Notes

Refer to Basic mitten recipe for full instructions.

4 colours of yarn used: base colour (white) and 3 contrast colours (brown, orange and purple).

Instructions

1. Cast on 72 sts.

2. Divide equally between 4 needles on first round (18 sts per needle).

3. Work cuff starting with Latvian Braid (see Cuff options) and following chart. Read chart from right to left and repeat twice.

4. Continue with stem and palm, following chart pattern.

5. When you reach the thumb position round, mark thumb over 16 sts, between the red lines.

6. When you reach the base of the shaping section, start decrease rounds.

7. Work thumb over 34 sts, repeating thumb section twice and working each additional corner stitch in background colour at the end of each repeat.

(Designed with reference to museum exhibit no: LM401)

Latvian Braid

Latvian Braid

36 sts

PINK SQUARES
MITTENS

Notes

Refer to Basic mitten recipe for full instructions.

3 colours of yarn used: base colour (black) and 2 contrast colours (light pink and dark pink).

Instructions

1. Cast on 72 sts.

2. Divide equally between 4 needles on first round (18 sts per needle).

3. Start cuff by knitting 7 rows with black. The embroidery detail is added later. Continue following the chart for colourwork section. Read chart from right to left and repeat twice.

4. Continue with stem and palm, following chart pattern.

5. When you reach the thumb position round, mark thumb over 16 sts, between the red lines.

6. When you reach the base of the shaping section, start decrease rounds.

7. Work thumb over 34 sts, repeating thumb section twice and working each additional corner stitch in background colour at the end of each repeat.

8. Use light pink yarn to add diagonal embroidery stitches around the cuff on the 6 rounds as shown in the chart.

(Designed with reference to museum exhibit no: CM/ML60885)

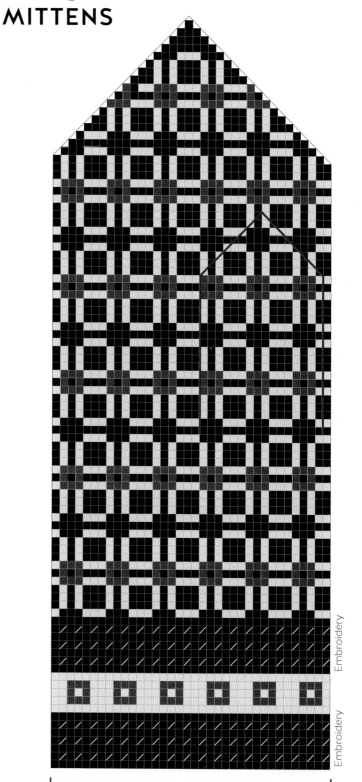

Embroidery

Embroidery

36 sts

ROWAN
MITTENS

Notes

Refer to Basic mitten recipe for full instructions.

4 colours of yarn used: base colour (black) and 3 contrast colours (dark blue, light blue and orange).

Instructions

1. Cast on 72 sts.

2. Divide equally between 4 needles on first round (18 sts per needle).

3. Start with The Notches method for the first 13 rounds (see Cuff options).

4. Continue with stem and palm, following chart pattern. Read chart from right to left and repeat twice.

5. When you reach the thumb position round, mark thumb over 16 sts, between the red lines.

6. When you reach the base of the shaping section, start decrease rounds.

7. Work thumb over 34 sts, repeating thumb section twice and working each additional corner stitch in background colour at the end of each repeat.

8. Use orange yarn to add textured embroidery stitches as follows: wrap yarn 3 times around each orange stitch.

(Designed with reference to museum exhibit no: CM/ML60863)

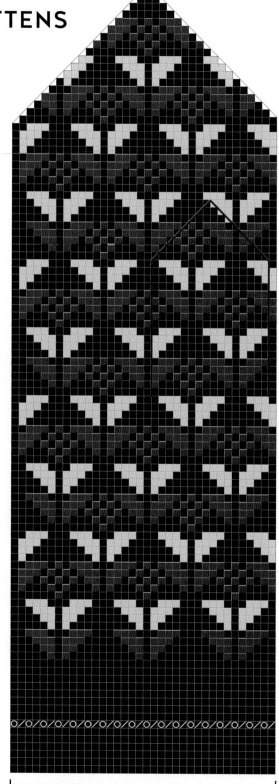

Fold here

36 sts

WHITE NET
MITTENS

Notes

Refer to Basic mitten recipe for full instructions.

4 colours of yarn used: base colour (black) and 3 contrast colours (white, green and light brown).

Instructions

1. Cast on 72 sts.

2. Divide equally between 4 needles on first round (18 sts per needle).

3. Start with The Notches method for the first 11 rounds (see Cuff options).

4. Continue with stem and palm, following chart pattern. Read chart from right to left and repeat twice.

5. When you reach the thumb position round, mark thumb over 14 sts, between the red lines.

6. When you reach the base of the shaping section, start decrease rounds.

7. Work thumb over 30 sts, repeating thumb section twice and working each additional corner stitch in background colour at the end of each repeat.

(Designed with reference to museum exhibit no: CM/ML60879)

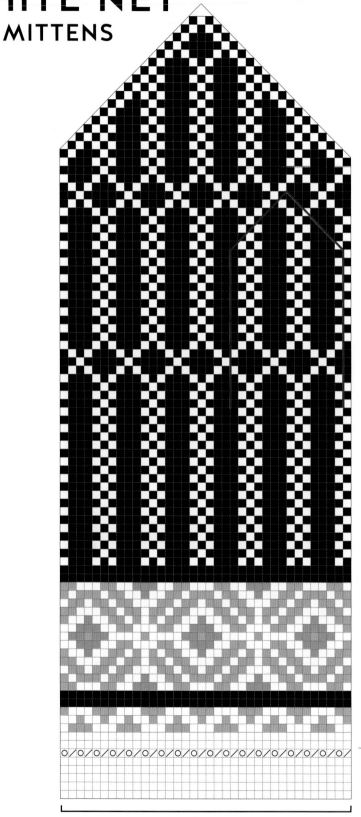

Fold here

36 sts

PEPPERMINT
MITTENS

Notes

Refer to Basic mitten recipe for full instructions.

4 colours of yarn used: base colour (light blue) and 3 contrast colours (teal, bright blue and white)

Instructions

1. Cast on 64 sts.

2. Divide equally between 4 needles on first round (16 sts per needle).

3. Start with The Notches method for the first 23 rounds (see Cuff options).

4. Continue with stem and palm, following chart pattern. Read chart from right to left and repeat twice.

5. When you reach the thumb position round, mark thumb over 14 sts, between the red lines.

6. When you reach the base of the shaping section, start decrease rounds.

7. Work thumb over 30 sts, repeating thumb section twice and working each additional corner stitch in background colour at the end of each repeat.

8. Use light blue yarn to add embroidery stitches around the top of the cuff as shown in the chart.

(Designed with reference to museum exhibit no: CM/ML60867)

Embroidery

Fold here

32 sts

LATVIAN QUILT
MITTENS

Notes

Refer to Basic mitten recipe for full instructions.

7 colours of yarn used: base colour (grey) and 6 contrast colours (black, brown, red, orange, yellow and white).

Instructions

1. Cast on 60 sts.

2. Divide equally between 4 needles on first round (15 sts per needle).

3. Start with (K1, P2) rib for 3 rounds.

4. Continue with stem and palm, following chart pattern. Read chart from right to left and repeat twice.

5. When you reach the thumb position round, mark thumb over 12 sts, between the red lines.

6. When you reach the base of the shaping section, start decrease rounds.

7. Work thumb over 26 sts, repeating thumb section twice and working each additional corner stitch in background colour at the end of each repeat.

(Designed with reference to museum exhibit no: CM/ML60886)

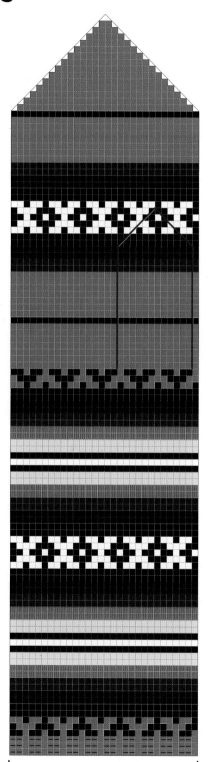

30 sts

WILD MINT
MITTENS

Notes

Refer to Basic mitten recipe for full instructions.

3 colours of yarn used: base colour (teal) and 2 contrast colours (light teal and white).

Instructions

1. Cast on 72 sts.

2. Divide equally between 4 needles on first round (18 sts per needle).

3. Start with (YO, K2tog, K2) rib for 30 rounds, changing colours as shown in the chart. Read chart from right to left and repeat twice.

4. Continue with stem and palm, following chart pattern.

5. Continue working in pattern, working the special stitch as follows: Holding the contrast colour loosely at the front of the work, knit 5 sts with the base colour. This will leave a long strand of colour. Work this for 5 rows as shown. On the 6th row, when knitting the centre stitch of the 5 sts, pull up the strands and work them together with the centre stitch.

6. When you reach the thumb position round, mark thumb over 14 sts, between the red lines.

7. When you reach the base of the shaping section, start decrease rounds.

8. Work thumb over 30 sts, repeating thumb section twice and working each additional corner stitch in background colour at the end of each repeat and working the decrease rounds in the base colour only.

(Designed with reference to museum exhibit no: CM/ML48311)

36 sts

BLUE SQUARES
MITTENS

Notes

Refer to Basic mitten recipe for full instructions.

3 colours of yarn used: base colour (beige) and 2 contrast colours (brown and blue).

Instructions

1. Cast on 64 sts.

2. Divide equally between 4 needles on first round (16 sts per needle).

3. Start with The Notches method for the first 23 rounds (see Cuff options).

4. Continue with stem and palm, following chart pattern. Read chart from right to left and repeat twice.

5. When you reach the thumb position round, mark thumb over 14 sts, between the red lines.

6. When you reach the base of the shaping section, start decrease rounds.

7. Work thumb over 30 sts, repeating thumb section twice and working each additional corner stitch in background colour at the end of each repeat.

(Designed with reference to museum exhibit no: CM/ML60860)

Fold here

32 sts

BRONZE AGE
MITTENS

Notes

Refer to Basic mitten recipe for full instructions.

3 colours of yarn used: base colour (orange) and 2 contrast colours (plum and lilac).

Instructions

1. Cast on 64 sts.

2. Divide equally between 4 needles on first round (16 sts per needle).

3. Work cuff following chart. Read chart from right to left and repeat twice.

4. Continue with stem and palm, following chart pattern.

5. Increase where indicated on chart. 66 sts.

6. When you reach the thumb position round, mark thumb over 14 sts, between the red lines.

7. When you reach the base of the shaping section, start decrease rounds.

8. Work thumb over 30 sts, repeating thumb section twice and working each additional corner stitch in background colour at the end of each repeat.

(Designed with reference to museum exhibit no: LM29704)

32 sts

CRYSTAL RAIN
MITTENS

Notes

Refer to Basic mitten recipe for full instructions.

6 colours of yarn used: base colour (black) and 5 contrast colours (green, orange, white, pink and blue).

Instructions

1. Cast on 64 sts.

2. Divide equally between 4 needles on first round (16 sts per needle).

3. Work cuff starting with Latvian Braid (see Cuff options) and following chart. Read chart from right to left and repeat twice.

4. Continue with stem and palm, following chart pattern.

6. When you reach the thumb position round, mark thumb over 14 sts, between the red lines.

7. When you reach the base of the shaping section, start decrease rounds.

8. Work thumb over 30 sts, repeating thumb section twice and working each additional corner stitch in background colour at the end of each repeat.

(Designed with reference to museum exhibit no: LM380)

Latvian Braid

Latvian Braid

Latvian Braid

32 sts

HAPPY DOTS
MITTENS

Notes

Refer to Basic mitten recipe for full instructions.

5 colours of yarn used: base colour (black) and 4 contrast colours (pink, beige, white and yellow).

Instructions

1. Cast on 72 sts using Pink.

2. Divide equally between 4 needles on first round (18 sts per needle).

3. Work cuff following chart. Read chart from right to left and repeat twice.

4. Continue with stem and palm, following chart pattern.

5. When you reach the thumb position round, mark thumb over 16 sts, between the red lines.

6. When you reach the base of the shaping section, start decrease rounds noting that some rounds work double decreases.

7. Work thumb over 34 sts, repeating thumb section twice and working each additional corner stitch in background colour at the end of each repeat.

(Designed with reference to museum exhibit no: LM463)

36 sts

STRANGE GAME
MITTENS

Notes

Refer to Basic mitten recipe for full instructions.

2 colours of yarn used: base colour (navy) and 1 contrast colour (white).

Instructions

1. Cast on 72 sts.

2. Divide equally between 4 needles on first round (18 sts per needle).

3. Start with the Simple Cuff method for the first 6 rounds (see Cuff options).

4. Continue with stem and palm, following chart pattern. Read chart from right to left and repeat twice.

5. When you reach the thumb position round, mark thumb over 16 sts, between the red lines.

6. When you reach the base of the shaping section, start decrease rounds.

7. Work thumb over 34 sts, repeating thumb section twice and working each additional corner stitch in background colour at the end of each repeat.

36 sts

DANCING FLOWERS
MITTENS

Notes

Refer to Basic mitten recipe for full instructions.

3 colours of yarn used: base colour (light grey) and 2 contrast colours (dark grey and pink).

Instructions

1. Cast on 64 sts.

2. Divide equally between 4 needles on first round (16 sts per needle).

3. Start with The Notches method for the first 11 rounds (see Cuff options).

4. Continue with stem and palm, following chart pattern. Read chart from right to left and repeat twice.

5. When you reach the thumb position round, mark thumb over 14 sts, between the black lines.

6. When you reach the base of the shaping section, start decrease rounds.

7. Work thumb over 30 sts, repeating thumb section twice and working each additional corner stitch in background colour at the end of each repeat.

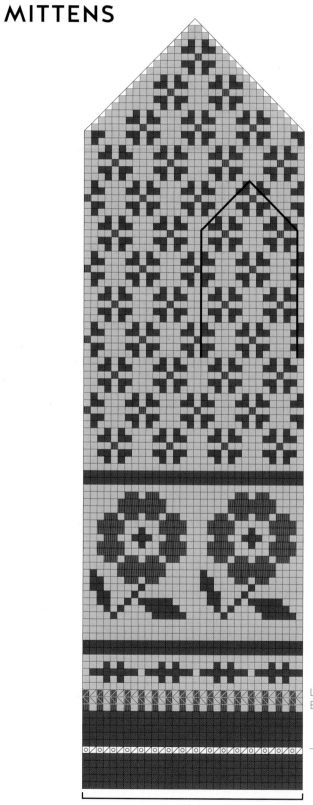

Latvian Braid

Fold here

32 sts

PEARL GREY
MITTENS

Notes

Refer to Basic mitten recipe for full instructions.

3 colours of yarn used: base colour (light grey) and 2 contrast colours (dark grey and pink).

Instructions

1. Cast on 64 sts.

2. Divide equally between 4 needles on first round (16 sts per needle).

3. Start with Simple Cuff method for the first 3 rounds (see Cuff options).

4. Continue with stem and palm, following chart pattern. Read mitten chart from right to left and repeat twice.

5. When you reach the thumb position round, mark thumb over 14 sts, between the black lines.

6. When you reach the base of the shaping section, start decrease rounds.

7. Work thumb over 30 sts, repeating thumb chart twice and working each additional corner stitch in background colour at the end of each repeat.

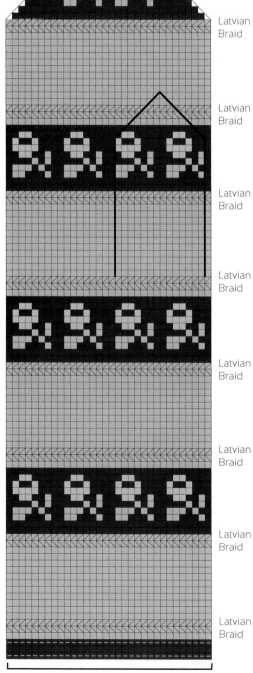

Latvian Braid

Latvian Braid

Latvian Braid

Latvian Braid

Latvian Braid

Latvian Braid

Latvian Braid

Latvian Braid

Thumb

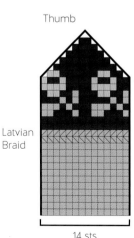

Latvian Braid

14 sts

32 sts

PEARL GREY MITTENS

PURPLE GAME
MITTENS

Notes

Refer to Basic mitten recipe for full instructions.

4 colours of yarn used: base colour (light grey) and 3 contrast colours (white, purple and pink).

Instructions

1. Cast on 72 sts.

2. Divide equally between 4 needles on first round (18 sts per needle).

3. Work cuff following charts and changing colours as shown. Read each chart from right to left.

4. Continue with stem and palm, following chart patterns.

5. Note that the front and back of mitten each have a separate chart.

6. When you reach the thumb position round, mark thumb over 17 sts, between the yellow lines.

7. When you reach the base of the shaping section, start decrease rounds.

8. Work thumb over 36 sts, repeating thumb section twice and working each additional corner stitch in background colour at the end of each repeat.

Back

Front

36 sts

SNOW DANCE
MITTENS

Notes

Refer to Basic mitten recipe for full instructions.

2 colours of yarn used: base colour (white) and 1 contrast colour (navy).

Instructions

1. Cast on 72 sts.

2. Divide equally between 4 needles on first round (18 sts per needle).

3. Work cuff following chart and changing colours as shown. Read chart from right to left and repeat twice.

4. Continue with stem and palm, following chart pattern.

5. When you reach the thumb position round, mark thumb over 15 sts, between the red lines.

6. When you reach the base of the shaping section, start decrease rounds.

7. Work thumb over 32 sts, repeating thumb section twice and working each additional corner stitch in background colour at the end of each repeat.

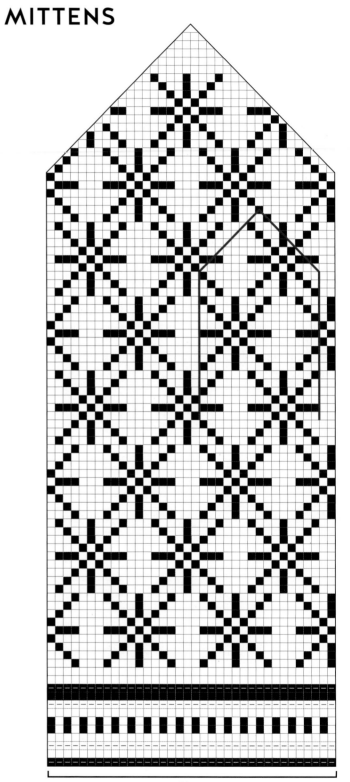

36 sts

TRICOLOR FLOWERS
MITTENS

Notes

Refer to Basic mitten recipe for full instructions.

6 colours of yarn used: base colour (grey) and 5 contrast colours (blue, dark pink, light pink, red and white).

Instructions

1. Cast on 72 sts.

2. Divide equally between 4 needles on first round (18 sts per needle).

3. Start with The Notches method for the first 11 rounds (see Cuff options).

4. Continue with stem and palm, following chart pattern. Read each chart from right to left.

5. Note that the front and back of mitten each have a separate chart.

6. When you reach the thumb position round, mark thumb over 16 sts, between the black lines.

7. When you reach the base of the shaping section, start decrease rounds.

8. Work thumb over 34 sts, repeating thumb section twice and working each additional corner stitch in background colour at the end of each repeat.

Back

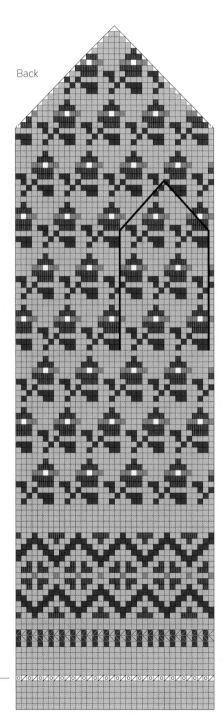

Front

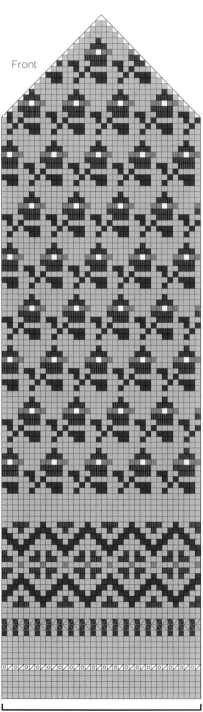

Fold here

36 sts

SHADES OF ROSES
MITTENS

Notes

Refer to Basic mitten recipe for full instructions.

4 colours of yarn used: base colour (light grey) and 3 contrast colours (dark grey, yellow and blue).

Instructions

1. Cast on 72 sts.

2. Divide equally between 4 needles on first round (18 sts per needle).

3. Start with The Notches method for the first 11 rounds (see Cuff options).

4. Continue with stem and palm, following chart pattern. Read each chart from right to left.

5. Note that the front and back of mitten each have a separate chart.

6. When you reach the thumb position round, mark thumb over 16 sts, between the yellow lines.

7. When you reach the base of the shaping section, start decrease rounds.

8. Work thumb over 34 sts, repeating thumb section twice and working each additional corner stitch in background colour at the end of each repeat.

Back

Front

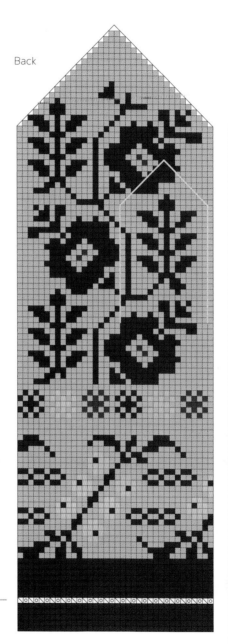

Fold here

36 sts

MIDNIGHT FLAKES
MITTENS

Notes

Refer to Basic mitten recipe for full instructions.

3 colours of yarn used: base colour (white) and 2 contrast colours (dark blue and red).

Instructions

1. Cast on 66 sts.

2. Divide between 4 needles on first round (16 sts on 1st and 3rd needle, 17 sts on 2nd and 4th per needle).

3. Work cuff following chart pattern. Read charts from right to left.

4. Continue with stem and palm, following chart pattern.

5. Note that the front and back of mitten each have a separate chart.

6. When you reach the thumb position round, mark thumb over 15 sts, between the red lines.

7. When you reach the base of the shaping section, start decrease rounds.

8. Work thumb over 32 sts, repeating thumb section twice and working each additional corner stitch in background colour at the end of each repeat.

Back

Front

33 sts

AUTUMN JOY
MITTENS

Notes

Refer to Basic mitten recipe for full instructions.

5 colours of yarn used: base colour (dark green) and 4 contrast colours (yellow, pink, orange and green).

Instructions

1. Cast on 72 sts.

2. Divide equally between 4 needles on first round (18 sts per needle).

3. Work cuff following chart. Read chart from right to left and repeat twice.

4. Continue with stem and palm, following chart pattern.

5. When you reach the thumb position round, mark thumb over 16 sts, between the red lines.

6. When you reach the base of the shaping section, start decrease rounds, noting that some rounds work double decreases.

7. Work thumb over 34 sts, repeating thumb section twice and working each additional corner stitch in background colour at the end of each repeat.

(Designed with reference to museum exhibit no: LM35290:2)

36 sts

GLASS TOWER
MITTENS

Notes

Refer to Basic mitten recipe for full instructions.

4 colours of yarn used: base colour (white) and 3 contrast colours (black, yellow and orange).

Instructions

1. Cast on 60 sts.

2. Divide equally between 4 needles on first round (16 sts per needle).

3. Start with The Notches method for the first 17 rounds (see Cuff options).

4. Continue with stem and palm, following chart pattern. Read chart from right to left and repeat twice.

5. When you reach the thumb position round, mark thumb over 14 sts, between the red lines.

6. When you reach the base of the shaping section, start decrease rounds.

7. Work thumb over 30 sts, repeating thumb section twice and working each additional corner stitch in background colour at the end of each repeat.

(Designed with reference to museum exhibit no: CM60877)

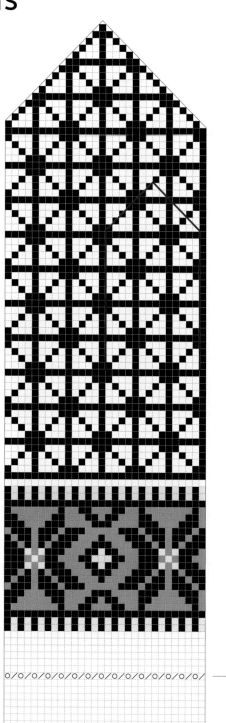

Fold here

30 sts

BERRY TIME
MITTENS

Notes

Refer to Basic mitten recipe for full instructions.

3 colours of yarn used: base colour (white) and 2 contrast colours (dark purple and light purple).

Instructions

1. Cast on 64 sts.

2. Divide equally between 4 needles on first round (16 sts per needle).

3. Work cuff following chart. Read chart from right to left and repeat twice.

4. Continue with stem and palm, following chart pattern.

5. Increase where indicated on chart. 66 sts.

6. When you reach the thumb position round, mark thumb over 14 sts, between the red lines.

7. When you reach the base of the shaping section, start decrease rounds.

8. Work thumb over 30 sts, repeating thumb section twice and working each additional corner stitch in background colour at the end of each repeat.

9. Use light purple yarn to add diagonal embroidery stitches around the top of the cuff as shown in the chart.

(Designed with reference to museum exhibit no: CM/ML60878)

Embroidery

32 sts

BLUE FLOWERBED
MITTENS

Notes

Refer to Basic mitten recipe for full instructions.

3 colours of yarn used: base colour (navy) and 2 contrast colours (blue and green).

Instructions

1. Cast on 66 sts.

2. Divide between 4 needles on first round (16 sts on 1st and 3rd needle, 17 sts on 2nd and 4th per needle).

3. Work cuff starting with Latvian Braid (see Cuff options) and following chart. Read chart from right to left and repeat twice.

4. Continue with stem and palm, following chart pattern.

6. When you reach the thumb position round, mark thumb over 13 sts, shown by the red line.

7. When you reach the base of the shaping section, start decrease rounds.

8. Work thumb over 28 sts, repeating thumb chart twice and working each additional corner stitch in background colour at the end of each repeat.

Thumb

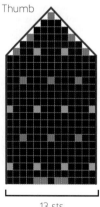

13 sts

Latvian Braid

Latvian Braid

33 sts

ORANGE JOE
MITTENS

Notes

Refer to Basic mitten recipe for full instructions.

3 colours of yarn used: base colour (white) and 2 contrast colours (navy and orange).

Instructions

1. Cast on 72 sts.

2. Divide equally between 4 needles on first round (18 sts per needle).

3. Start with The Notches method for the first 11 rounds (see Cuff options).

4. Continue with stem and palm, following chart pattern. Read each mitten chart from right to left.

5. Note that the front and back of mitten each have a separate chart.

6. When you reach the thumb position round, mark thumb over 16 sts, between the green lines.

7. When you reach the base of the shaping section, start decrease rounds.

8. Work thumb over 34 sts, repeating thumb section twice and working each additional corner stitch in background colour at the end of each repeat.

Fold here

36 sts

BACK IN THE 60s
MITTENS

Notes

Refer to Basic mitten recipe for full instructions.

3 colours of yarn used: base colour (white) and 2 contrast colours (black and orange).

Instructions

1. Cast on 72 sts.

2. Divide equally between 4 needles on first round (18 sts per needle).

3. Start with (P2, K2) rib for the first 10 rounds.

4. Continue with stem and palm, following chart pattern. Read chart from right to left and repeat twice.

5. When you reach the thumb position round, mark thumb over 16 sts, between the green lines.

6. When you reach the base of the shaping section, start decrease rounds.

7. Work thumb over 34 sts, repeating thumb section twice and working each additional corner stitch in background colour at the end of each repeat.

36 sts

PINK FLOWERBED
MITTENS

Notes

Refer to Basic mitten recipe for full instructions.

3 colours of yarn used: base colour (purple) and 2 contrast colours (pink and white).

Instructions

1. Cast on 66 sts.

2. Divide between 4 needles on first round (16 sts on 1st and 3rd needle, 17 sts on 2nd and 4th per needle).

3. Work cuff starting with Latvian Braid (see Cuff options) and following chart. Read chart from right to left and repeat twice.

4. Continue with stem and palm, following chart pattern.

6. When you reach the thumb position round, mark thumb over 15 sts, shown by the red line.

7. When you reach the base of the shaping section, start decrease rounds.

8. Work thumb over 32 sts, repeating thumb chart twice and working each additional corner stitch in background colour at the end of each repeat.

Latvian Braid

Latvian Braid

33 sts

Thumb

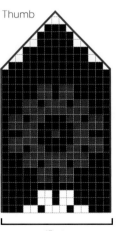

15 sts

ROMANCE
GLOVES

Notes

Refer to Basic glove recipe for full instructions.

5 colours of yarn used: base colour (white), and 4 contrast colours (dark green, black, beige and light green).

Instructions

1. Cast on 64 sts.

2. Divide equally between 4 needles on first round (16 sts per needle).

3. Start with The Notches method for the first 19 rounds (see Cuff options).

4. Continue following chart until the thumb position row. Read chart from right to left and repeat twice.

5. Mark thumb with scrap yarn.

6. Continue following chart until you have reached the beginning of the little finger.

7. Work glove fingers with base colour and maintain the textured pattern.

8. Work thumb with base colour and maintain the textured pattern.

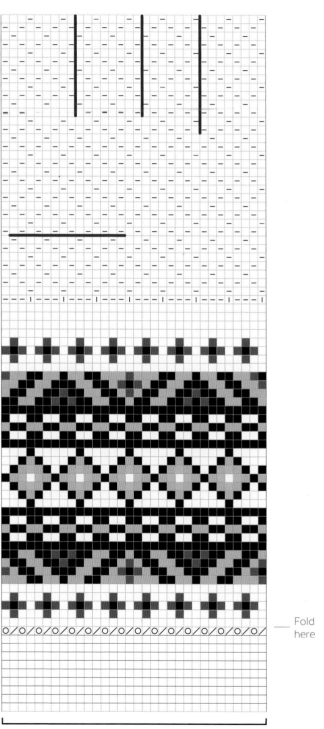

Fold here

32 sts

SOFT PINK
GLOVES

Notes

Refer to Basic glove recipe for full instructions.

3 colours of yarn used: base colour (purple), and 2 contrast colours (pink and white).

Instructions

1. Cast on 72 sts.

2. Divide equally between 4 needles on first round (18 sts per needle).

3. Work cuff following chart. Read chart from right to left and repeat twice.

4. Continue following chart until the thumb position row.

5. Mark thumb with scrap yarn.

6. Continue, following chart until you have reached the beginning of the little finger.

7. Work glove fingers with base colour.

8. Work thumb with base colour.

36 sts

(Designed with reference to museum exhibit no: LM35291)

DOMINOES
GLOVES

Notes

Refer to Basic glove recipe for full instructions.

4 colours of yarn used: base colour (white), and 3 contrast colours (red, green and black).

Instructions

1. Cast on 72 sts.

2. Divide equally between 4 needles on first round (18 sts per needle).

3. Work cuff following chart. Read chart from right to left and repeat twice.

4. Continue following chart until the thumb position row.

5. Mark thumb with scrap yarn.

6. Continue, following chart until you have reached the beginning of the little finger.

7. Work glove fingers while maintaining the colourwork pattern.

8. Work thumb while maintaining the colourwork pattern.

36 sts

(Designed with reference to museum exhibit no: LM397)

GINGERBREAD
GLOVES

Notes

Refer to Basic glove recipe for full instructions.

4 colours of yarn used: base colour (brown), and 3 contrast colours (white, orange and beige).

Instructions

1. Cast on 72 sts.

2. Divide equally between 4 needles on first round (18 sts per needle).

3. Work cuff following chart. Read chart from right to left and repeat twice.

4. Continue following chart until the thumb position row.

5. Mark thumb with scrap yarn.

6. Continue, following chart until you have reached the beginning of the little finger.

7. Work glove fingers while maintaining the colourwork pattern.

8. Work thumb while maintaining the colourwork pattern.

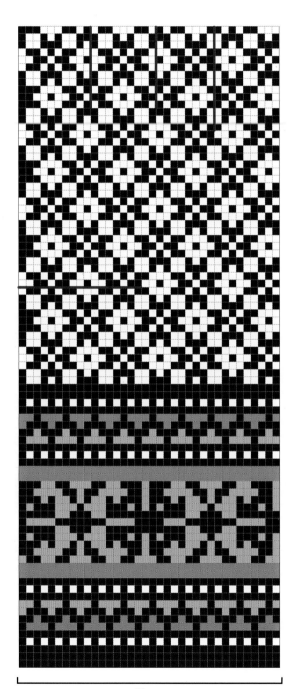

36 sts

HALLOWEEN
GLOVES

Notes

Refer to Basic glove recipe for full instructions.

4 colours of yarn used: base colour (black), and 3 contrast colours (orange, white and blue).

Instructions

1. Cast on 64 stitches.

2. Divide equally between 4 needles on first round (16 sts per needle).

3. Start with the Simple Cuff method for the first 4 rounds (see Cuff options), changing colours as indicated in chart. Read chart from right to left and repeat twice.

4. Continue following chart until the thumb position row.

5. Mark thumb with scrap yarn.

6. Continue following chart until you have reached the beginning of the little finger.

7. Work glove fingers with base colour.

8. Work thumb with base colour.

32 sts

(Designed with reference to museum exhibit no: LM18205)

SPRING FLOWERS
GLOVES

Notes

Refer to Basic glove recipe for full instructions.

4 colours of yarn used: base colour (dark brown), and 3 contrast colours (white, pink and green).

Instructions

1. Cast on 72 sts.

2. Divide equally between 4 needles on first round (18 sts per needle).

3. Start with the Simple Cuff method for the first 2 rounds (see Cuff options), Read chart from right to left and repeat twice.

4. Continue following chart until the thumb position row.

5. Mark thumb with scrap yarn.

6. Continue, following chart until you have reached the beginning of the little finger.

7. Work glove fingers with base colour.

8. Work thumb with base colour.

36 sts

(Designed with reference to museum exhibit no: LM404)

WINTER SUN
MITTENS

Notes

Refer to Basic mitten recipe for full instructions.

2 colours of yarn used: base colour (white) and 1 contrast colour (dark grey).

Instructions

1. Cast on 72 sts.

2. Divide equally between 4 needles on first round (18 sts per needle).

3. Start with The Notches method for the first 11 rounds (see Cuff options).

4. Continue with stem and palm, following chart pattern. Read mitten chart from right to left and repeat twice.

5. When you reach the thumb position round, mark thumb over 16 sts, between the red lines.

6. When you reach the base of the shaping section, start decrease rounds.

7. Work thumb over 34 sts, repeating thumb chart twice and working each additional corner stitch in background colour at the end of each repeat.

Thumb

16 sts

36 sts

Fold here

WINTER SUN
FINGERLESS MITTENS

Notes

Refer to Fingerless recipes for full instructions.

2 colours of yarn used: base colour (dark grey) and 1 contrast colour (white).

Instructions

1. Cast on 72 sts.

2. Divide equally between 4 needles on first round (18 sts per needle).

3. Start with the Simple Cuff method for the first 6 rounds (see Cuff options).

4. Continue with stem and palm, following chart pattern. Read chart from right to left and repeat twice.

5. When you reach the thumb position round, mark thumb over 16 sts, between the red lines.

6. Continue following chart until you complete the upper cuff. End with Simple Cuff for 6 rounds, then cast off all sts.

7. Work thumb over 34 sts, repeating thumb chart twice and working each additional corner stitch in background colour at the end of each repeat. End with Simple Cuff for 6 rounds, then cast off thumb sts.

Thumb

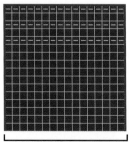

16 sts

36 sts

MORNING STAR
MITTENS

Notes

Refer to Basic mitten recipe for full instructions.

2 colours of yarn used: base colour (white) and 1 contrast colour (black).

Instructions

1. Cast on 72 sts.

2. Divide equally between 4 needles on first round (18 sts per needle).

3. Start with The Notches method for the first 11 rounds (see Cuff options).

4. Continue with stem and palm, following chart patterns. Read each mitten chart from right to left.

5. When you reach the thumb position round, mark thumb over 16 sts, between the red lines.

6. When you reach the base of the shaping section, start decrease rounds.

7. Work thumb over 34 sts, repeating thumb chart twice and working each additional corner stitch in background colour at the end of each repeat.

Back

Front

Thumb

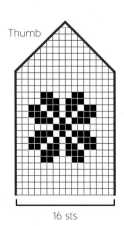

16 sts

36 sts

Fold here

MORNING STAR
WRIST WARMERS

Notes

Refer to Fingerless recipes for full instructions.

2 colours of yarn used: base colour (black) and 1 contrast colour (white).

Instructions

1. Cast on 72 sts.

2. Divide equally between 4 needles on first round (18 sts per needle).

3. Start and end with (P1, K1) rib for 3 rounds.

4. Follow chart pattern for centre section. Read chart from right to left and repeat twice.

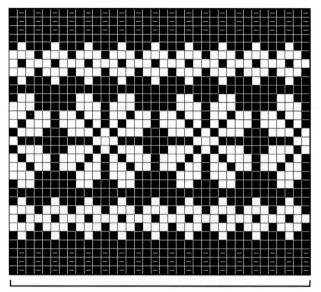

36 sts

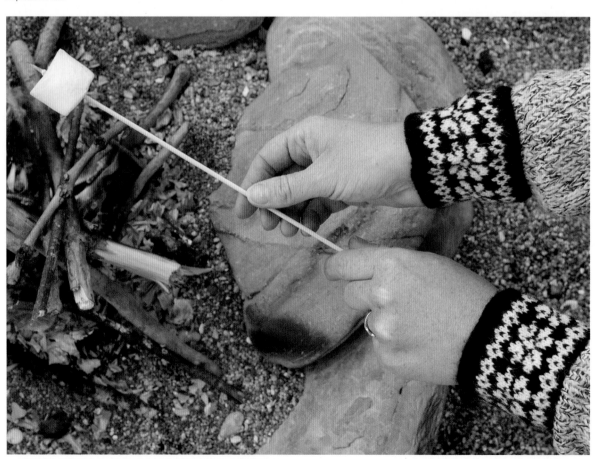

LITTLE HEARTS
WRIST WARMERS

Notes

Refer to Fingerless recipes for full instructions.

3 colours of yarn used: base colour (dark grey) and 2 contrast colours (grey and red).

Instructions

1. Cast on 72 sts.

2. Divide equally between 4 needles on first round (18 sts per needle).

3. Start with The Fringe method (see Cuff options).

4. Follow chart pattern for centre section. Read chart from right to left and repeat twice.

5. Work Latvian Braid where indicated on chart.

6. Increase and decrease where indicated on chart.

7. End with Simple Cuff for 5 rounds (see Cuff options).

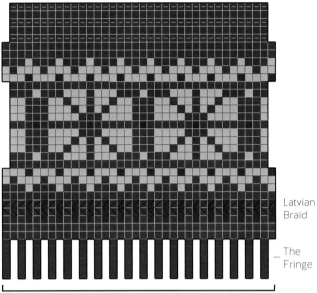

Latvian Braid

The Fringe

36 sts

WINTER HOLIDAY
MITTENS

Notes

Refer to Basic mitten recipe for full instructions.

3 colours of yarn used: base colour (white) and 2 contrast colours (black and red).

Instructions

1. Cast on 72 sts.

2. Divide equally between 4 needles on first round (18 sts per needle).

3. Start with The Notches method for the first 11 rounds (see Cuff options).

4. Continue with stem and palm, following chart pattern. Read mitten chart from right to left and repeat twice.

5. When you reach the thumb position round, mark thumb over 16 sts, between the red lines.

6. When you reach the base of the shaping section, start decrease rounds.

7. Work thumb over 34 sts, repeating thumb section twice and working each additional corner stitch in background colour at the end of each repeat.

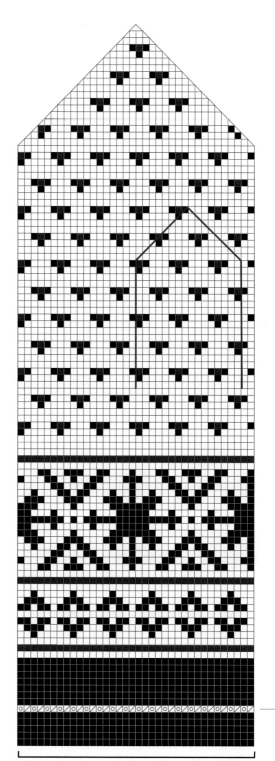

Fold here

36 sts

WINTER HOLIDAY
FINGERLESS MITTENS

Notes

Refer to Fingerless recipes for full instructions.

3 colours of yarn used: base colour (white) and 2 contrast colours (black and red).

Instructions

1. Cast on 72 sts.

2. Divide equally between 4 needles on first round (18 sts per needle).

3. Start and end with (K1, P1) rib for 4 rounds.

4. Continue with stem and palm, following chart pattern. Read chart from right to left and repeat twice.

5. When you reach the thumb position round, mark thumb over 16 sts, between the red lines.

6. Continue following chart until you complete the upper cuff. End with (K1, P1) rib for 4 rounds, then cast off all sts.

7. Work thumb over 34 sts, repeating thumb chart twice and working each additional corner stitch in background colour at the end of each repeat. End with (K1, P1) rib for 4 rounds, then cast off thumb sts.

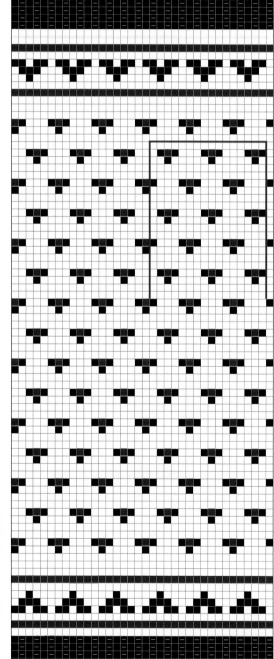

Thumb

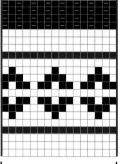

16 sts

36 sts

WINDMILL
MITTENS

Notes

Refer to Basic mitten recipe for full instructions.

3 colours of yarn used: base colour (white) and 2 contrast colours (black and red).

Instructions

1. Cast on 72 sts.

2. Divide equally between 4 needles on first round (18 sts per needle).

3. Start with The Notches method for the first 11 rounds (see Cuff options).

4. Work Latvian Braid where indicated on chart (see Cuff options).

5. Continue with stem and palm, following chart pattern. Read mitten chart from right to left and repeat twice.

6. When you reach the thumb position round, mark thumb over 16 sts, between the red lines.

7. When you reach the base of the shaping section, start decrease rounds.

8. Work thumb over 34 sts, repeating thumb section twice and working each additional corner stitch in background colour at the end of each repeat.

Latvian Braid

Fold here

36 sts

WINDMILL
FINGERLESS MITTENS

Notes

Refer to Fingerless recipes for full instructions.

3 colours of yarn used: base colour (white) and 2 contrast colours (black and red).

Instructions

1. Cast on 72 sts.

2. Divide equally between 4 needles on first round (18 sts per needle).

3. Start and end with a Simple Cuff for 5 rounds (see Cuff options).

4. Continue with stem and palm, following chart pattern. Read chart from right to left and repeat twice.

5. Work Latvian Braid where indicated on chart (see Cuff options).

6. When you reach the thumb position round, mark thumb over 16 sts, between the red lines.

7. Continue following chart until you complete the upper cuff. End with a Simple Cuff for 6 rounds, then cast off all sts.

8. Work thumb over 34 sts, repeating thumb chart twice and working each additional corner stitch in background colour at the end of each repeat. End with a Simple Cuff for 6 rounds, then cast off thumb sts.

Latvian Braid

Latvian Braid

Latvian Braid

Thumb

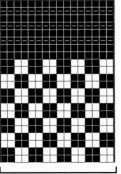

16 sts

36 sts

GREY NET
MITTENS

Notes

Refer to Basic mitten recipe for full instructions.

4 colours of yarn used: base colour (grey) and 3 contrast colours (dark grey, white and red).

Instructions

1. Cast on 72 sts.

2. Divide equally between 4 needles on first round (18 sts per needle).

3. Start with The Notches method for the first 11 rounds (see Cuff options).

4. Continue with stem and palm, following chart pattern. Read mitten chart from right to left and repeat twice.

5. When you reach the thumb position round, mark thumb over 16 sts, between the red lines.

6. When you reach the base of the shaping section, start decrease rounds.

7. Work thumb over 34 sts, repeating thumb section twice and working each additional corner stitch in background colour at the end of each repeat.

Fold here

36 sts

LUCKY SCALES
MITTENS

Notes

Refer to Basic mitten recipe for full instructions.

4 colours of yarn used: base colour (light grey) and 3 contrast colours (dark grey, white and black).

Instructions

1. Cast on 72 sts.

2. Divide equally between 4 needles on first round (18 sts per needle)

3. Start with The Notches method for the first 11 rounds (see Cuff options).

4. Continue with stem and palm, following chart pattern. Read mitten chart from right to left and repeat twice.

5. Work Latvian Braid where indicated on chart (see Cuff options).

6. When you reach the thumb position round, mark thumb over 16 sts, between the red lines.

7. When you reach the base of the shaping section, start decrease rounds.

8. Work thumb over 34 sts, repeating thumb section twice and working each additional corner stitch in background colour at the end of each repeat.

Latvian Braid

Fold here

36 sts

LITTLE HEARTS
MITTENS

Notes

Refer to Basic mitten recipe for full instructions.

3 colours of yarn used: base colour (dark grey) and 2 contrast colours (light grey and red).

Instructions

1. Cast on 68 sts.

2. Divide equally between 4 needles on first round (17 sts per needle).

3. Start with The Notches method for the first 11 rounds (see Cuff options).

4. Continue with stem and palm, following chart patterns. Read each mitten chart from right to left.

5. Note that the front and back of mitten each have a separate chart.

6. Increase and decrease where indicated on charts.

7. When you reach the thumb position round, mark thumb over 15 sts, between the red lines.

8. When you reach the base of the shaping section, start decrease rounds.

9. Work thumb over 32 sts, repeating thumb section twice and working each additional corner stitch in background colour at the end of each repeat.

Back

Front

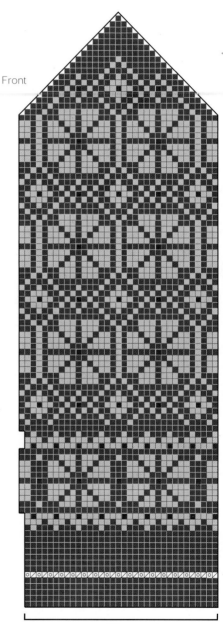

Fold here

34 sts

LITTLE HEARTS
FINGERLESS MITTENS

Notes

Refer to Basic mitten recipe for full instructions.

3 colours of yarn used: base colour (light grey) and 2 contrast colours (dark grey and red).

Instructions

1. Cast on 68 sts.

2. Divide equally between 4 needles on first round (17 sts per needle).

3. Start and end with the Simple Cuff method for 6 rounds (see Cuff options).

4. Continue with stem and palm, following chart patterns. Read each chart from right to left.

5. Note that the front and back of mitten each have a separate chart.

6. Work Latvian Braid where indicated on charts (see Cuff options).

7. Increase and decrease where indicated on charts.

8. When you reach the thumb position round, mark thumb over 14 sts, between the red lines.

9. Continue following charts until you complete the upper Simple Cuff for 6 rounds, then cast off all sts.

10. Work thumb over 30 sts, repeating thumb chart twice and working each additional corner stitch in background colour at the end of each repeat. End with a Simple Cuff for 6 rounds, then cast off thumb sts.

Back

Front

Latvian Braid

Latvian Braid

Latvian Braid

34 sts

Thumb

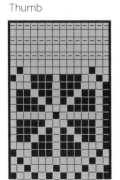

14 sts

WEEKDAY
MITTENS

Notes

Refer to Basic mitten recipe for full instructions.

2 colours of yarn used: base colour (light grey) and 1 contrast colour (dark grey).

Instructions

1. Cast on 72 sts.

2. Divide equally between 4 needles on first round (18 sts per needle).

3. Start with The Notches method for the first 11 rounds (see Cuff options).

4. Continue with stem and palm, following chart pattern. Read mitten chart from right to left and repeat twice.

5. When you reach the thumb position round, mark thumb over 16 sts, between the red lines.

6. When you reach the base of the shaping section, start decrease rounds.

7. Work thumb over 34 sts, repeating thumb section twice and working each additional corner stitch in background colour at the end of each repeat.

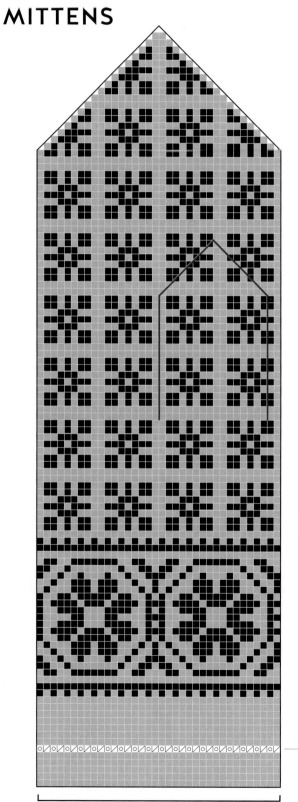

Fold here

36 sts

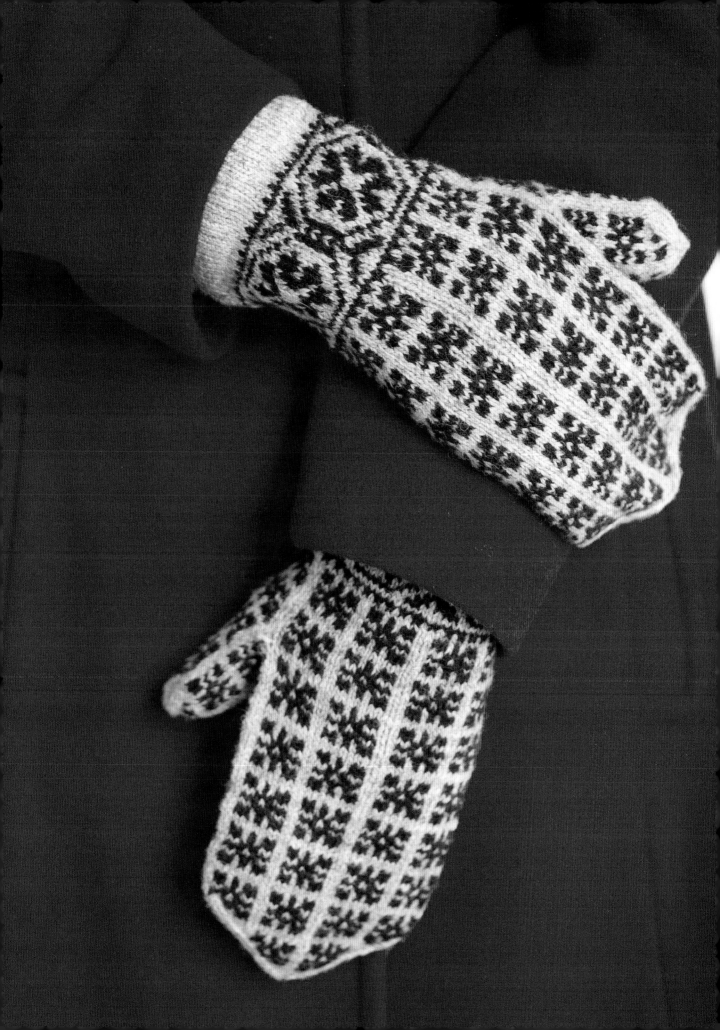

WEEKDAY
FINGERLESS MITTENS

Notes

Refer to Fingerless recipes for full instructions.

2 colours of yarn used: base colour (dark grey) and 1 contrast colour (light grey).

Instructions

1. Cast on 72 sts.

2. Divide equally between 4 needles on first round (18 sts per needle).

3. Start with the Simple Cuff method for the first 6 rounds (see Cuff options).

4. Continue with stem and palm, following chart pattern. Read chart from right to left and repeat twice.

5. When you reach the thumb position round, mark thumb over 17 sts, between the red lines.

6. Continue following chart until you complete the upper cuff. End with Simple Cuff for 5 rounds, then cast off all sts.

7. Work thumb over 36 sts, repeating thumb chart twice and working each additional corner stitch in background colour at the end of each repeat. End with Simple Cuff for 5 rounds, then cast off thumbs sts.

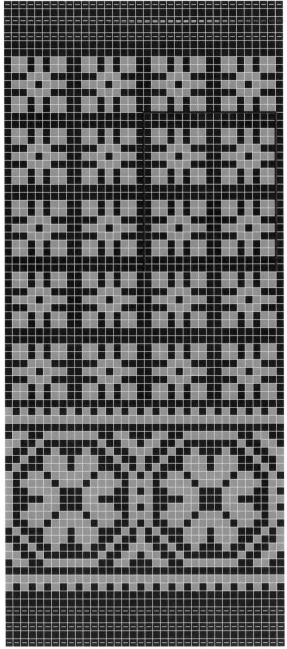

Thumb

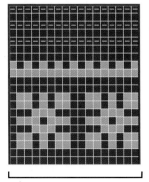

17 sts

36 sts

MARA
MITTENS

Notes

Refer to Basic mitten recipe for full instructions.

3 colours of yarn used: base colour (black) and 2 contrast colours (white and red).

Instructions

1. Cast on 72 sts.

2. Divide equally between 4 needles on first round (18 sts per needle).

3. Start with The Notches method for the first 11 rounds (see Cuff options).

4. Continue with stem and palm, following chart patterns. Read each mitten chart from right to left.

5. Note that the front and back of mitten each have a separate chart.

6. When you reach the thumb position round, mark thumb over 16 sts, between the red lines.

7. When you reach the base of the shaping section, start decrease rounds.

8. Work thumb over 34 sts, repeating thumb section twice and working each additional corner stitch in background colour at the end of each repeat.

Back

Front

Fold here

36 sts

MARA
FINGERLESS MITTENS

Notes

Refer to Fingerless recipes for full instructions.

3 colours of yarn used: base colour (black) and 2 contrast colours (white and red).

Instructions

1. Cast on 72 sts.

2. Divide equally between 4 needles on first round (18 sts per needle).

3. Start with The Notches method for the first 7 rounds (see Cuff options).

4. Continue with stem and palm, following chart patterns. Read each chart from right to left.

5. Note that the front and back of mitten each have a separate chart.

6. Work Latvian Braid where indicated on charts (see Cuff options).

7. When you reach the thumb position round, mark thumb over 16 sts, between the red lines.

8. Continue following charts until you complete the upper cuff. End with Simple Cuff for 5 rounds (see Cuff options), then cast off all sts.

9. Work thumb over 34 sts, repeating thumb chart twice and working each additional corner stitch in background colour at the end of each repeat. End with Simple Cuff for 5 rounds, then cast off thumb sts.

Back

Front

Latvian Braid

Latvian Braid

Latvian Braid

36 sts

Thumb

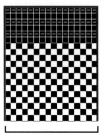

16 sts

GREY ACORNS
MITTENS

Notes

Refer to Basic mitten recipe for full instructions.

4 colours of yarn used: base colour (dark grey) and 3 contrast colours (grey, white and red).

Instructions

1. Cast on 72 sts.

2. Divide equally between 4 needles on first round (18 sts per needle).

3. Start with The Notches method for the first 11 rounds (see Cuff options).

4. Continue with stem and palm, following chart pattern. Read mitten chart from right to left and repeat twice.

5. When you reach the thumb position round, mark thumb over 16 sts, between the red lines.

6. When you reach the base of the shaping section, start decrease rounds.

7. Work thumb over 34 sts, repeating thumb section twice and working each additional corner stitch in background colour at the end of each repeat.

Fold here

36 sts

GREY ACORNS
FINGERLESS MITTENS

Notes

Refer to Fingerless recipes for full instructions.

4 colours of yarn used: base colour (black) and 3 contrast colours (grey, white and red).

Instructions

1. Cast on 72 sts.

2. Divide equally between 4 needles on first round (18 sts per needle).

3. Start with The Notches method for the first 7 rounds (see Cuff options), working just 3 rounds either side of the foldline.

4. Continue with stem and palm, following chart pattern. Read chart from right to left and repeat twice.

5. Work Latvian Braid where indicated on chart (see Cuff options).

6. When you reach the thumb position round, mark thumb over 16 sts, between the red lines.

7. Continue following chart until you complete the upper cuff. End with Simple Cuff for 5 rounds (see Cuff options), then cast off all sts.

8. Work thumb over 34 sts, repeating thumb chart twice and working each additional corner stitch in background colour at the end of each repeat. End with Simple Cuff for 5 rounds, then cast off thumb sts.

Latvian Braid

Fold here

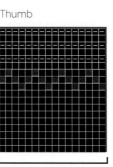

Thumb

16 sts

36 sts

LITTLE DOTS
MITTENS

Notes

Refer to Basic mitten recipe for full instructions.

4 colours of yarn used: base colour (dark grey) and 3 contrast colours (grey, white and red).

Instructions

1. Cast on 72 sts.

2. Divide equally between 4 needles on first round (18 sts per needle).

3. Start with The Notches method for the first 11 rounds (see Cuff options).

4. Work Latvian Braid where indicated on chart (see Cuff options).

5. Continue with stem and palm, following chart patterns. Read each mitten chart from right to left.

6. Note that the front and back of mitten each have a separate chart.

7. Decrease where indicated on charts.

8. When you reach the thumb position round, mark thumb over 16 sts, between the black lines.

9. When you reach the base of the shaping section, start decrease rounds.

10. Work thumb over 34 sts, repeating thumb section twice and working each additional corner stitch in background colour at the end of each repeat.

Back

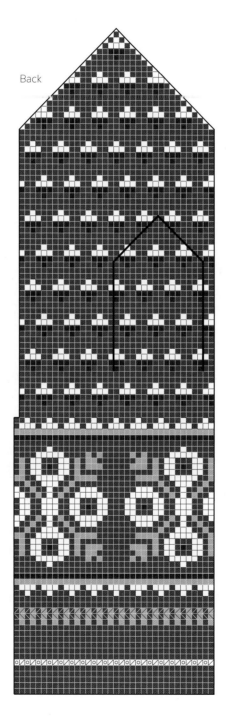

Front

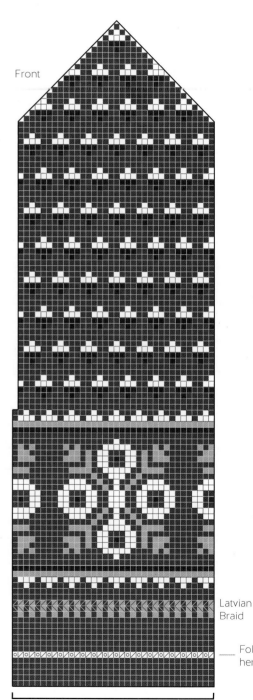

Latvian Braid

— Fold here

36 sts

LITTLE DOTS
FINGERLESS MITTENS

Notes

Refer to Fingerless recipes for full instructions.

4 colours of yarn used: base colour (dark grey) and 3 contrast colours (grey, white and red).

Instructions

1. Cast on 72 sts.

2. Divide equally between 4 needles on first round (18 sts per needle).

3. Start with the Simple Cuff method for the first 5 rounds (see Cuff options).

4. Continue with stem and palm, following chart pattern. Read chart from right to left and repeat twice.

5. Decrease where indicated on chart.

6. When you reach the thumb position round, mark thumb over 15 sts, between the black lines.

7. Continue following chart until you complete the upper cuff. End with Simple Cuff for 5 rounds (see Cuff options), then cast off all sts.

8. Work thumb over 32 sts, repeating thumb chart twice and working each additional corner stitch in background colour at the end of each repeat. End with Simple Cuff for 5 rounds, then cast off thumb sts.

Thumb

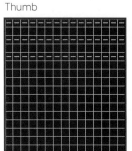

15 sts

36 sts

WHITE & WISE
MITTENS

Notes

Refer to Basic mitten recipe for full instructions.

2 colours of yarn used: base colour (white) and 1 contrast colour (blue).

Instructions

1. Cast on 72 sts.

2. Divide equally between 4 needles on first round (18 sts per needle).

3. Start with the Simple Cuff method for the first 6 rounds (see Cuff options).

4. Continue with stem and palm, following chart pattern. Read mitten chart from right to left and repeat twice.

5. When you reach the thumb position round, mark thumb over 16 sts, between the red lines.

6. When you reach the base of the shaping section, start decrease rounds.

7. Work thumb over 34 sts, repeating thumb section twice and working each additional corner stitch in background colour at the end of each repeat.

36 sts

WHITE & WISE
FINGERLESS MITTENS

Notes

Refer to Fingerless recipes for full instructions.

2 colours of yarn used: base colour (blue) and 1 contrast colour (white).

Instructions

1. Cast on 72 sts.

2. Divide equally between 4 needles on first round (18 sts per needle).

3. Start with (P1, K1) rib for the first 6 rounds.

4. Continue with stem and palm, following chart pattern. Read chart from right to left and repeat twice.

5. When you reach the thumb position round, mark thumb over 16 sts, between the red lines.

6. Continue following chart until you complete the upper cuff. End with (P1, K1) rib for 6 rounds, then cast off all sts.

7. Work thumb over 34 sts, repeating thumb chart twice and working each additional corner stitch in background colour at the end of each repeat. End with (P1, K1) rib for 6 rounds, then cast off thumb sts.

36 sts

Thumb

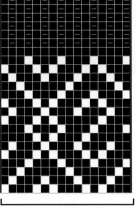

16 sts

SNOWBALL
MITTENS

Notes

Refer to Basic mitten recipe for full instructions.

2 colours of yarn used: base colour (blue) and 1 contrast colour (white).

Instructions

1. Cast on 70 sts.

2. Divide between 4 needles on first round (17 sts on 1st and 3rd needles, 18 sts on 2nd and 4th needles).

3. Start with the Simple Cuff method for the first 6 rounds (see Cuff options).

4. Continue with stem and palm, following chart patterns. Read each mitten chart from right to left.

5. Note that the front and back of mitten each have a separate chart.

6. When you reach the thumb position round, mark thumb over 15 sts, between the red lines.

7. When you reach the base of the shaping section, start decrease rounds.

8. Work thumb over 32 sts, repeating thumb section twice and working each additional corner stitch in background colour at the end of each repeat.

Back

Front

35 sts

SNOWBALL
FINGERLESS MITTENS

Notes

Refer to Fingerless recipes for full instructions.

2 colours of yarn used: base colour (white) and 1 contrast colour (blue).

Instructions

1. Cast on 70 sts.

2. Divide between 4 needles on first round (17 sts on 1st and 3rd needles, 18 sts on 2nd and 4th needles).

3. Start with the Simple Cuff method for the first 6 rounds (see Cuff options).

4. Continue with stem and palm, following chart patterns. Read each chart from right to left and

5. Note that the front and back of mitten each have a separate chart.

6. When you reach the thumb position round, mark thumb over 15 sts, between the red lines.

7. Continue following charts until you complete the upper cuff. End with Simple Cuff for 6 rounds, then cast off all sts.

8. Work thumb over 32 sts, repeating thumb chart twice and working each additional corner stitch in background colour at the end of each repeat. End with Simple Cuff for 5 rounds, then cast off thumb sts.

Back

Front

35 sts

Thumb

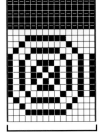

15 sts

CROSSROADS
MITTENS

Notes

Refer to Basic mitten recipe for full instructions.

3 colours of yarn used: base colour (blue) and 2 contrast colours (white and red).

Instructions

1. Cast on 72 sts.

2. Divide equally between 4 needles on first round (18 sts per needle).

3. Start with the Simple Cuff method for the first 6 rounds (see Cuff options).

4. Continue with stem and palm, following chart pattern. Read mitten chart from right to left and repeat twice.

5. When you reach the thumb position round, mark thumb over 16 sts, between the red lines.

6. When you reach the base of the shaping section, start decrease rounds.

7. Work thumb over 34 sts, repeating thumb section twice and working each additional corner stitch in background colour at the end of each repeat.

36 sts

ORANGE SUN
MITTENS

Notes

Refer to Basic mitten recipe for full instructions.

4 colours of yarn used: base colour (orange) and 3 contrast colours (white, blue and light orange).

Instructions

1. Cast on 68 sts.

2. Divide equally between 4 needles on first round (17 sts per needle).

3. Start with The Notches method for the first 11 rounds (see Cuff options).

4. Continue with stem and palm, following chart patterns. Read each mitten chart from right to left.

5. Note that the front and back of mitten each have a separate chart.

6. Increase where indicated on charts.

7. When you reach the thumb position round, mark thumb over 15 sts, between the blue lines.

8. When you reach the base of the shaping section, start decrease rounds.

9. Work thumb over 32 sts, repeating thumb section twice and working each additional corner stitch in background colour at the end of each repeat.

Back

Front

Fold here

34 sts

SNOW FLOWER
MITTENS

Notes

Refer to Basic mitten recipe for full instructions.

5 colours of yarn used: base colour (black) and 4 contrast colours (white, blue, red and green),

Instructions

1. Cast on 64 sts.

2. Divide equally between 4 needles on first round (16 sts per needle).

3. Start with The Notches method for the first 11 rounds (see Cuff options).

4. Continue with stem and palm, following chart pattern. Read mitten chart from right to left and repeat twice.

5. When you reach the thumb position round, mark thumb over 14 sts, between the red lines.

6. When you reach the base of the shaping section, start decrease rounds.

7. Work thumb over 30 sts, repeating thumb section twice and working each additional corner stitch in background colour at the end of each repeat.

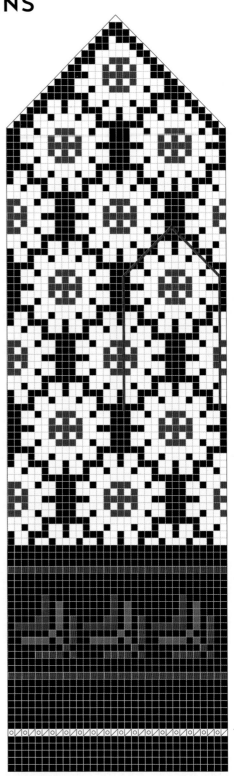

Fold here

32 sts

SNOW FLOWER
FINGERLESS MITTENS

Notes

Refer to Fingerless recipes for full instructions.

4 colours of yarn used: base colour (black) and 3 contrast colours (white, blue and orange).

Instructions

1. Cast on 64 sts.

2. Divide equally between 4 needles on first round (16 sts per needle).

3. Start with (K1, P1) rib for the first 6 rounds.

4. Continue with stem and palm, following chart pattern. Read chart from right to left and repeat twice.

5. When you reach the thumb position round, mark thumb over 14 sts, between the red lines.

6. Continue following chart until you complete the upper cuff. End with (K1, P1) rib for 6 rounds, then cast off all sts.

7. Work thumb over 30 sts, repeating thumb chart twice and working each additional corner stitch in background colour at the end of each repeat. End with (K1, P1) rib for 6 rounds, then cast off thumb sts.

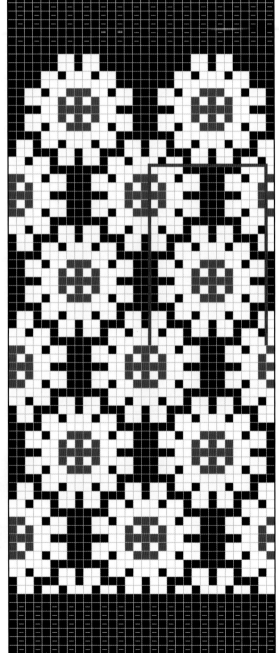

Thumb

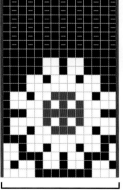

14 sts

32 sts

AUTUMN LEAVES
MITTENS

Notes

Refer to Basic mitten recipe for full instructions.

5 colours of yarn used: base colour (black) and 4 contrast colours (yellow, blue, green and red).

Instructions

1. Cast on 72 sts.

2. Divide equally between 4 needles on first round (18 sts per needle).

3. Start with The Notches method for the first 11 rounds (see Cuff options).

4. Continue with stem and palm, following chart pattern. Read mitten chart from right to left and repeat twice.

5. When you reach the thumb position round, mark thumb over 16 sts, between the red lines.

6. When you reach the base of the shaping section, start decrease rounds.

7. Work thumb over 34 sts, repeating thumb section twice and working each additional corner stitch in background colour at the end of each repeat.

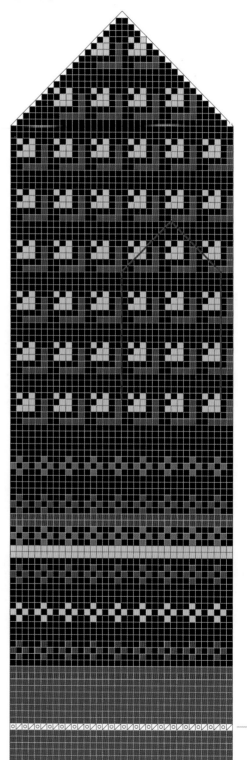

Fold here

36 sts

FESTIVE
MITTENS

Notes

Refer to Basic mitten recipe for full instructions.

6 colours of yarn used: base colour (black) and 5 contrast colours (yellow, blue, turquoise, pink and red).

Instructions

1. Cast on 84 sts.

2. Divide equally between 4 needles on first round (21 sts per needle).

3. Start with The Fringe method (see Cuff options).

4. Continue with stem and palm, following chart patterns. Read each mitten chart from right to left.

5. Note that the front and back of mitten each have a separate chart.

6. Decrease where indicated on charts.

7. When you reach the thumb position round, mark thumb over 16 sts, between the white lines.

8. When you reach the base of the shaping section, start decrease rounds.

9. Work thumb over 34 sts, repeating thumb chart twice and working each additional corner stitch in background colour at the end of each repeat.

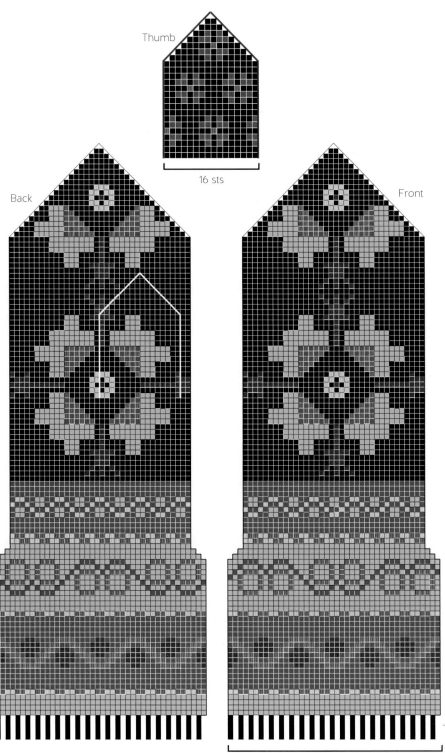

FESTIVE
WRIST WARMERS

Notes

Refer to Fingerless recipes for full instructions.

6 colours of yarn used: base colour (black) and 5 contrast colours (yellow, blue, turquoise, pink and red).

Instructions

1. Cast on 72 sts.

2. Divide equally between 4 needles on first round (18 sts per needle).

3. Start and end with the Simple Cuff method for 5 rounds (see Cuff options).

4. Follow chart pattern for centre section. Read chart from right to left and repeat twice.

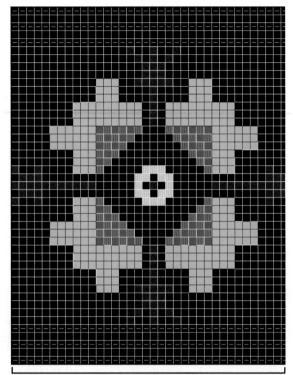

36 sts

BLUE STAR
WRIST WARMERS

Notes

Refer to Fingerless recipes for full instructions.

5 colours of yarn used: base colour (black) and 4 contrast colours (yellow, blue, green and red).

Instructions

1. Cast on 72 sts.

2. Divide equally between 4 needles on first round (18 sts per needle).

3. Start and end with the Simple Cuff method for 5 rounds in colours indicated on chart (see Cuff options).

4. Follow chart pattern for centre section. Read chart from right to left and repeat twice.

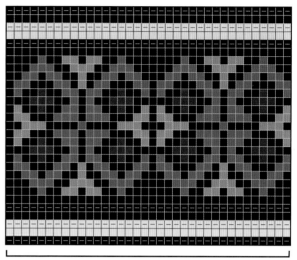

36 sts

BLUE STAR
MITTENS

Notes

Refer to Basic mitten recipe for full instructions.

6 colours of yarn used: base colour (black) and 5 contrast colours (yellow, blue, orange, green and red).

Instructions

1. Cast on 72 sts.

2. Divide equally between 4 needles on first round (18 sts per needle).

3. Start with The Notches method for the first 11 rounds (see Cuff options).

4. Work Latvian Braid where indicated on chart (see Cuff options).

5. Continue with stem and palm, following chart pattern. Read mitten chart from right to left and repeat twice.

6. When you reach the thumb position round, mark thumb over 16 sts, between the white lines.

7. When you reach the base of the shaping section, start decrease rounds.

8. Work thumb over 34 sts, repeating thumb section twice and working each additional corner stitch in background colour at the end of each repeat.

Latvian Braid

Fold here

36 sts

MIDNIGHT FOREST
MITTENS

Notes

Refer to Basic mitten recipe for full instructions.

5 colours of yarn used: base colour (black) and 4 contrast colours (yellow, blue, pale blue and green).

Instructions

1. Cast on 64 sts.

2. Divide equally between 4 needles on first round (16 sts per needle).

3. Start with The Notches method for the first 11 rounds (see Cuff options).

4. Continue with stem and palm, following chart pattern. Read mitten chart from right to left and repeat twice.

5. When you reach the thumb position round, mark thumb over 14 sts, between the white lines.

6. When you reach the base of the shaping section, start decrease rounds.

7. Work thumb over 30 sts, repeating thumb chart twice and working each additional corner stitch in background colour at the end of each repeat.

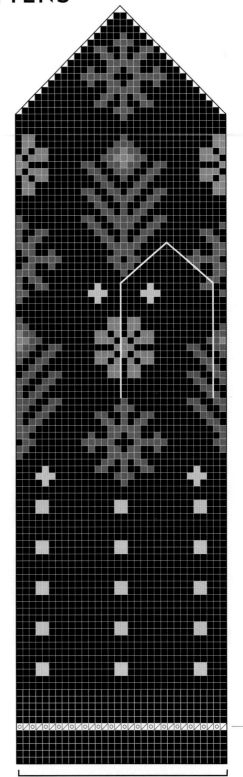

Thumb

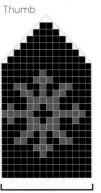

Fold here

14 sts

32 sts

BRIGHT LIGHTS
MITTENS

Notes

Refer to Basic mitten recipe for full instructions.

5 colours of yarn used: base colour (black) and 4 contrast colours (yellow, blue, pink and green)

Instructions

1. Cast on 72 sts.

2. Divide equally between 4 needles on first round (18 sts per needle).

3. Start with The Notches method for the first 11 rounds (see Cuff options).

4. Continue with stem and palm, following chart pattern. Read mitten chart from right to left and repeat twice.

5. When you reach the thumb position round, mark thumb over 16 sts, between the white lines.

6. When you reach the base of the shaping section, start decrease rounds.

7. Work thumb over 34 sts, repeating thumb section twice and working each additional corner stitch in background colour at the end of each repeat.

Fold here

36 sts

PINK CROCUS
MITTENS

Notes

Refer to Basic mitten recipe for full instructions.

3 colours of yarn used: base colour (white) and 2 contrast colours (pink and green).

Instructions

1. Cast on 64 sts.

2. Divide equally between 4 needles on first round (16 sts per needle).

3. Start with The Notches method for the first 11 rounds (see Cuff options).

4. Continue with stem and palm, following chart pattern. Read mitten chart from right to left and repeat twice.

5. When you reach the thumb position round, mark thumb over 14 sts, between the black lines.

6. When you reach the base of the shaping section, start decrease rounds.

7. Work thumb over 30 sts, repeating thumb section twice and working each additional corner stitch in background colour at the end of each repeat.

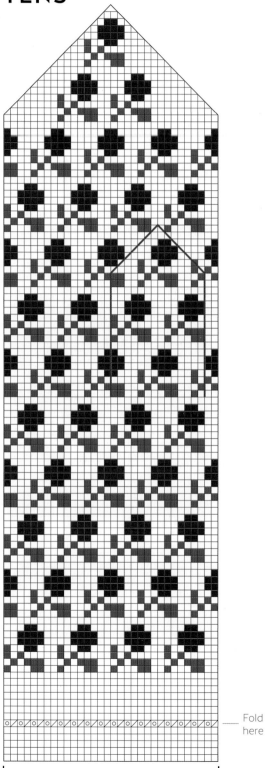

Fold here

32 sts

PINK CROCUS
FINGERLESS MITTENS

Notes

Refer to Fingerless recipes for full instructions.

3 colours of yarn used: base colour (black) and 2 contrast colours (pink and green).

Instructions

1. Cast on 64 sts.

2. Divide equally between 4 needles on first round (16 sts per needle).

3. Start with (K1, P1) rib for the first 5 rounds.

4. Continue with stem and palm, following chart pattern. Read chart from right to left and repeat twice.

5. When you reach the thumb position round, mark thumb over 14 sts, between the white lines.

6. Continue following chart until you complete the upper cuff. End with (K1, P1) rib for 5 rounds, then cast off all sts.

7. Work thumb over 30 sts, repeating thumb chart twice and working each additional corner stitch in background colour at the end of each repeat. End with (K1, P1) rib for 5 rounds, then cast off thumb sts.

Thumb

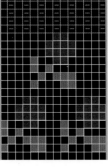

14 sts

32 sts

AZALEA
MITTENS

Notes

Refer to Basic mitten recipe for full instructions.

3 colours of yarn used: base colour (white) and 2 contrast colours (pink and green).

Instructions

1. Cast on 72 sts.

2. Divide equally between 4 needles on first round (18 sts per needle).

3. Start with The Notches method for the first 11 rounds (see Cuff options).

4. Continue with stem and palm, following chart pattern. Read mitten chart from right to left and repeat twice.

5. When you reach the thumb position round, mark thumb over 16 sts, between the black lines.

6. When you reach the base of the shaping section, start decrease rounds.

7. Work thumb over 34 sts, repeating thumb section twice and working each additional corner stitch in background colour at the end of each repeat.

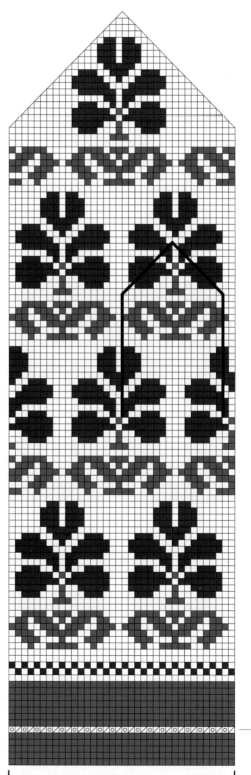

Fold here

36 sts

AZALEA
FINGERLESS MITTENS

Notes

Refer to Fingerless recipes for full instructions.

3 colours of yarn used: base colour (black) and 2 contrast colours (pink and green).

Instructions

1. Cast on 72 sts.

2. Divide equally between 4 needles on first round (18 sts per needle).

3. Start with (K1, P1) rib for the first 5 rounds.

4. Continue with stem and palm, following chart pattern. Read chart from right to left and repeat twice.

5. When you reach the thumb position round, mark thumb over 16 sts, between the white lines.

6. Continue following chart until you complete the upper cuff. End with (K1, P1) rib for 5 rounds, then cast off all sts.

7. Work thumb over 34 sts, repeating thumb chart twice and working each additional corner stitch in background colour at the end of each repeat. End with (K1, P1) rib for 5 rounds, then cast off thumb sts.

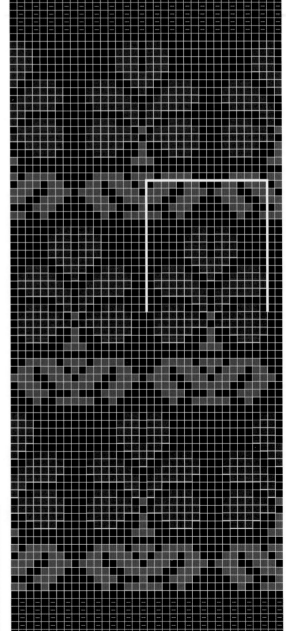

Thumb

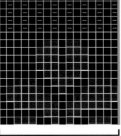

16 sts

36 sts

PURPLE ROSES
MITTENS

Notes

Refer to Basic mitten recipe for full instructions.

4 colours of yarn used: base colour (black) and 3 contrast colours (purple, red and green).

Instructions

1. Cast on 72 sts.

2. Divide equally between 4 needles on first round (18 sts per needle).

3. Start with The Notches method for the first 11 rounds (see Cuff options).

4. Continue with stem and palm, following chart pattern. Read mitten chart from right to left and repeat twice.

5. When you reach the thumb position round, mark thumb over 16 sts, between the white lines.

6. When you reach the base of the shaping section, start decrease rounds.

7. Work thumb over 34 sts, repeating thumb section twice and working each additional corner stitch in background colour at the end of each repeat.

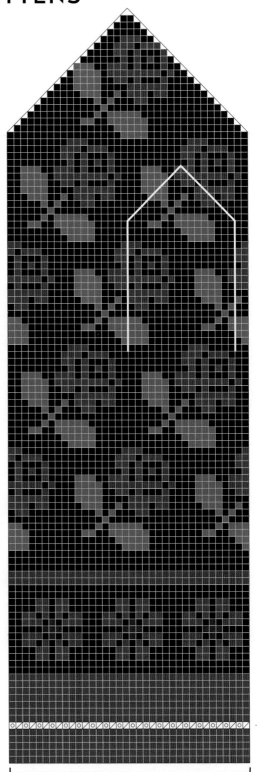

Fold here

36 sts

PURPLE ROSES
FINGERLESS MITTENS

Notes

Refer to Fingerless recipes for full instructions.

3 colours of yarn used: base colour (black) and 2 contrast colours (purple and green).

Instructions

1. Cast on 72 sts.

2. Divide equally between 4 needles on first round (18 sts per needle).

3. Start with (K1, P1) rib for 5 rounds.

4. Continue with stem and palm, following chart pattern. Read chart from right to left and repeat twice.

5. When you reach the thumb position round, mark thumb over 16 sts, between the red lines.

6. Continue following chart until you complete the upper cuff. End with (K1, P1) rib for 5 rounds, then cast off all sts.

7. Work thumb over 34 sts, repeating thumb chart twice and working each additional corner stitch in background colour at the end of each repeat. End with (K1, P1) rib for 5 rounds, then cast off thumb sts.

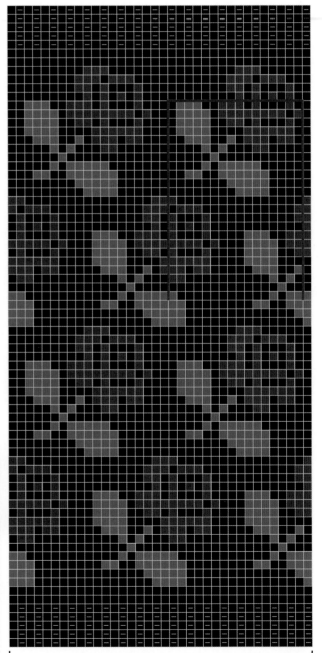

Thumb

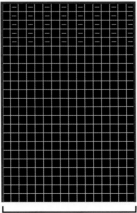

16 sts

36 sts

FLOWER GARDEN
MITTENS

Notes

Refer to Basic mitten recipe for full instructions.

5 colours of yarn used: base colour (black) and 4 contrast colours (purple, red, yellow and green).

Instructions

1. Cast on 72 sts.

2. Divide equally between 4 needles on the first round (18 sts per needle)

3. Start with The Notches method for the first 11 rounds (see Cuff options).

4. Continue with stem and palm, following chart patterns. Read each mitten chart from right to left and decrease where indicated on chart.

5. Note that the front and back of mitten each have a separate chart.

6. When you reach the thumb position round, mark thumb over 16 sts, between the white lines.

7. When you reach the base of the shaping section, start decrease rounds.

8. Work thumb over 34 sts, repeating thumb chart twice and working each additional corner stitch in background colour at the end of each repeat.

Thumb

16 sts

Back

Front

36 sts

Fold here

CRANBERRIES
MITTENS

Notes

Refer to Basic mitten recipe for full instructions.

4 colours of yarn used: base colour (black) and 3 contrast colours (red, green and brown).

Instructions

1. Cast on 72 sts.

2. Divide equally between 4 needles on first round (18 sts per needle).

3. Start with The Notches method for the first 11 rounds (see Cuff options).

4. Continue with stem and palm, following chart pattern. Read mitten chart from right to left and repeat twice.

5. When you reach the thumb position round, mark thumb over 16 sts, between the white lines.

6. When you reach the base of the shaping section, start decrease rounds.

7. Work thumb over 34 sts, repeating thumb section twice and working each additional corner stitch in background colour at the end of each repeat.

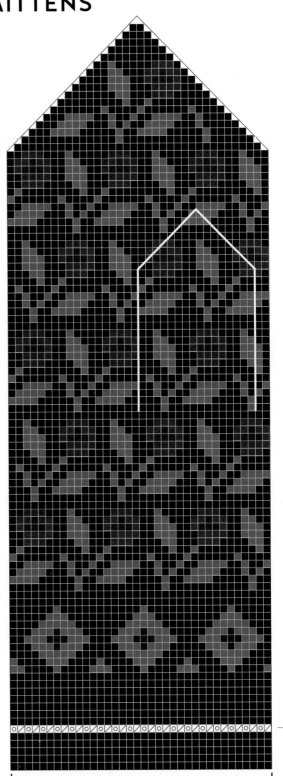

Fold here

36 sts

RED ROSES
MITTENS

Notes

Refer to Basic mitten recipe for full instructions.

4 colours of yarn used: base colour (black) and 3 contrast colours (red, green and brown).

Instructions

1. Cast on 72 sts.

2. Divide equally between 4 needles on first round (18 sts per needle).

3. Start with The Notches method for the first 11 rounds (see Cuff options).

4. Continue with stem and palm, following chart pattern. Read mitten chart from right to left and repeat twice.

5. When you reach the thumb position round, mark thumb over 16 sts, between the white lines.

6. When you reach the base of the shaping section, start decrease rounds.

7. Work thumb over 34 sts, repeating thumb section twice and working each additional corner stitch in background colour at the end of each repeat.

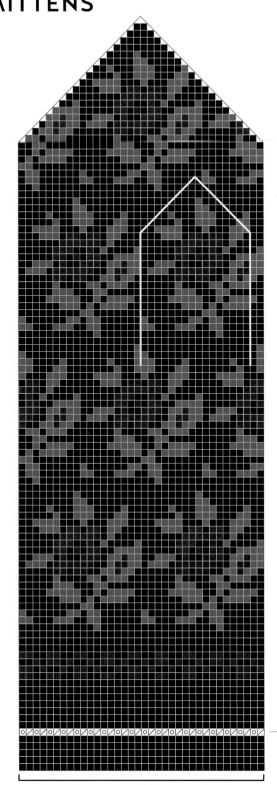

Fold here

36 sts

RED ROSES
WRIST WARMERS

Notes

Refer to Fingerless recipes for full instructions.

4 colours of yarn used: base colour (black) and 3 contrast colours (red, green and dark red).

Instructions

1. Cast on 72 sts.

2. Divide equally between 4 needles on first round (18 sts per needle).

3. Start and end with the Simple Cuff method for 5 rounds (see Cuff options), changing colour as indicated on chart.

4. Follow chart pattern for centre section. Read chart from right to left and repeat twice.

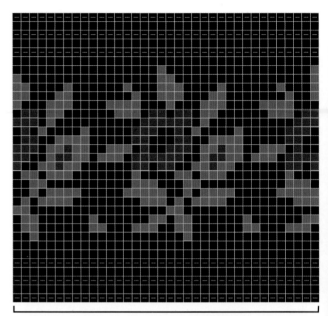

36 sts

CHRISTMAS STARS
WRIST WARMERS

Notes

Refer to Fingerless recipes for full instructions.

3 colours of yarn used: base colour (black) and 2 contrast colours (red and green).

Instructions

1. Cast on 72 sts.

2. Divide equally between 4 needles on first round (18 sts per needle).

3. Start and end with the Simple Cuff method for 3 rounds (see Cuff options).

4. Follow chart pattern for centre section. Read chart from right to left and repeat twice.

5. Work Latvian Braid where indicated on chart (see Cuff options).

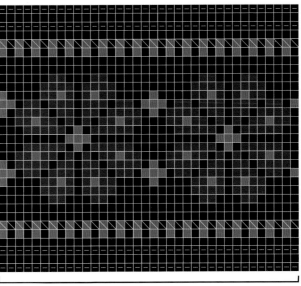

Latvian Braid

Latvian Braid

36 sts

POPPY FIELD
MITTENS

Notes

Refer to Basic mitten recipe for full instructions.

4 colours of yarn used: base colour (black) and 3 contrast colours (red, green and yellow)

Instructions

1. Cast on 72 sts.

2. Divide equally between 4 needles on first round (18 sts per needle).

3. Start with The Notches method for the first 11 rounds (see Cuff options).

4. Continue with stem and palm, following chart pattern. Read mitten chart from right to left and repeat twice.

5. When you reach the thumb position round, mark thumb over 16 sts, between the white lines.

6. When you reach the base of the shaping section, start decrease rounds.

7. Work thumb over 34 sts, repeating thumb section twice and working each additional corner stitch in background colour at the end of each repeat.

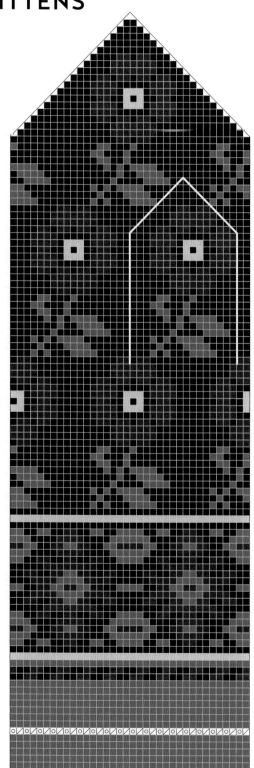

Fold here

36 sts

CHRISTMAS STARS
MITTENS

Notes

Refer to Basic mitten recipe for full instructions.

3 colours of yarn used: base colour (black) and 2 contrast colours (red and green).

Instructions

1. Cast on 72 sts.

2. Divide equally between 4 needles on first round (18 sts per needle).

3. Start with The Notches method for the first 11 rounds (see Cuff options).

4. Continue with stem and palm, following chart pattern. Read mitten chart from right to left and repeat twice.

5. When you reach the thumb position round, mark thumb over 16 sts, between the white lines.

6. When you reach the base of the shaping section, start decrease rounds.

7. Work thumb over 34 sts, repeating thumb section twice and working each additional corner stitch in background colour at the end of each repeat.

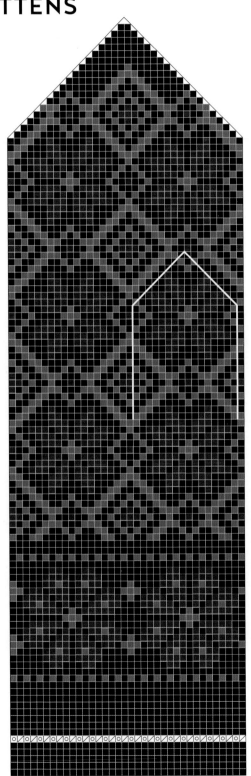

Fold here

36 sts

CHRISTMAS FLOWER
MITTENS

Notes

Refer to Basic mitten recipe for full instructions.

3 colours of yarn used: base colour (black) and 2 contrast colours (red and green).

Instructions

1. Cast on 72 sts.

2. Divide equally between 4 needles on first round (18 sts per needle).

3. Start with The Notches method for the first 11 rounds (see Cuff options).

4. Continue with stem and palm, following chart pattern. Read mitten chart from right to left and repeat twice.

5. Decrease where indicated on chart.

6. When you reach the thumb position round, mark thumb over 15 sts, between the white lines.

7. When you reach the base of the shaping section, start decrease rounds.

8. Work thumb over 32 sts, repeating thumb chart twice and working each additional corner stitch in background colour at the end of each repeat.

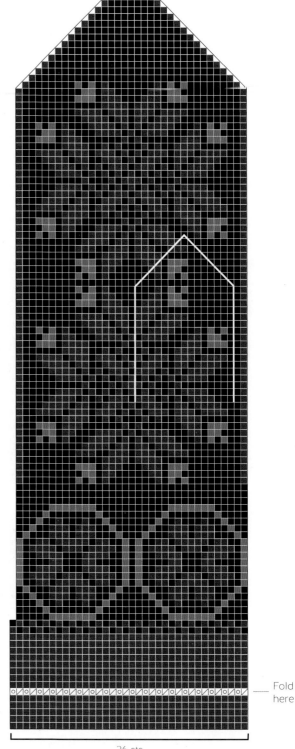

Fold here

36 sts

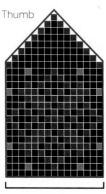

Thumb

15 sts

MARA
GLOVES

Notes

Refer to Basic glove recipe for full instructions.

5 colours of yarn used: base colour (light grey), and 4 contrast colours (green, navy, yellow and red).

Instructions

1. Cast on 72 sts.

2. Divide equally between 4 needles on first round (18 sts per needle).

3. Work cuff following charts. Read each chart from right to left.

4. Continue following charts until the thumb position row.

5. Note that the front and back of glove each have a separate chart.

6. Where indicated on chart, decrease by 1st with k2tog at the end of 2nd and 4th needle. 70 sts

7. Where indicated on chart, increase by 1st with M1 at the end of 2nd and 4th needle. 72 sts

8. Mark thumb with scrap yarn.

9. Continue following charts until you have reached the beginning of the little finger.

10. Work glove fingers with base colour.

11. Work thumb with base colour.

Back

Front

36 sts

TOUCH OF PINK
FINGERLESS MITTENS

Notes

Refer to Basic mitten recipe for full instructions.

2 colours of yarn used: base colour (dark grey), and 1 contrast colour (pink).

Instructions

1. Cast on 72 sts.

2. Divide equally between 4 needles on first round (18 sts per needle).

3. Work cuff starting with Latvian Braid (see Cuff options) following charts. Read each chart from right to left.

4. Note that the front and back of glove each have a separate chart.

5. Continue following charts until the thumb position row.

6. Mark thumb over 16 sts, between white lines.

7. Continue following charts until you have reached the upper joint of the little finger.

8. Work Latvian Braid, then cast off all sts.

9. Work thumb over 36 sts, repeating thumb section twice and working each additional corner stitch in background colour at the end of each repeat.

10. Cast off thumb sts.

Back

Front

36 sts

WHITE & RED
GLOVES

Notes

Refer to Basic glove recipe for full instructions.

4 colours of yarn used: base colour (white), and 3 contrast colours (beige, red and black).

Instructions

1. Cast on 72 sts.

2. Divide equally between 4 needles on first round (18 sts per needle).

3. Work cuff following charts. Read each chart from right to left.

4. Note that the front and back of glove each have a separate chart.

5. Continue following charts until the thumb position row.

6. Mark thumb with scrap yarn.

7. Continue knitting, following charts until you have reached the beginning of the little finger.

8. Work glove fingers with base colour.

9. Work thumb with base colour.

Back

Front

36 sts

BLUE DOTS
FINGERLESS MITTENS

Notes

Refer to Fingerless recipes for full instructions.

3 colours of yarn used: base colour (beige), and 2 contrast colours (blue and dark brown).

Instructions

1. Cast on 72 sts.

2. Divide equally between 4 needles on first round (18 sts per needle).

3. Work cuff following charts. Read each chart from right to left.

4. Note that the front and back of mitten each have a separate chart.

5. Where indicated on chart, decrease by 1st with k2tog at the end of 2nd and 4th needle. 70 sts

6. Continue following charts until the thumb position row.

7. Mark thumb over 13 sts between yellow lines.

8. Continue following charts until you have reached the upper joint of the little finger.

9. Work Latvian Braid (see Cuff options) following charts, then cast off all sts.

10. Work thumb over 28 sts, repeating thumb chart twice and working each additional corner stitch in background colour at the end of each repeat.

11. Work Latvian Braid following thumb chart, then cast off thumb sts.

Back

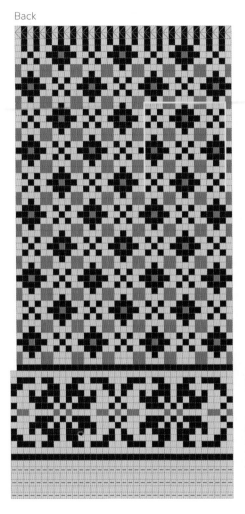

Front

Lat
Bra

36 sts

Thumb

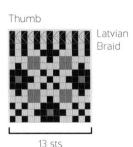

Latvian
Braid

13 sts

LIGHT DECOR
FINGERLESS GLOVES

Notes

Refer to Fingerless recipes for full instructions.

2 colours of yarn used: base colour (brown), and 1 contrast colour (beige).

Instructions

1. Cast on 72 sts.

2. Divide equally between 4 needles on first round (18 sts per needle).

3. Work cuff following charts. Read each chart from right to left.

4. On round 9 work (k2tog, YO) all round to create a fold line, then work 8 more rounds.

5. On round 18 fold the cuff at the fold line with cast-on edge inside. For each stitch, pick up a loop from the cast on edge with the left needle and knit this together with the stitch.

6. Continue following charts, with colour pattern on 1st and 2nd needle for right hand glove and on 3rd and 4th needle for left hand glove. Knit the stitches on the other two needles with base colour.

7. Note that the front and back of glove each have a separate chart.

8. Continue following charts until the thumb position row.

9. Mark thumb with scrap yarn.

10. Continue following chart until you have reached the beginning of the little finger.

11. Work glove fingers with base colour.

12. Knit each finger until it reaches the upper joint of your finger, then cast off.

13. Work thumb with base colour.

Back Front

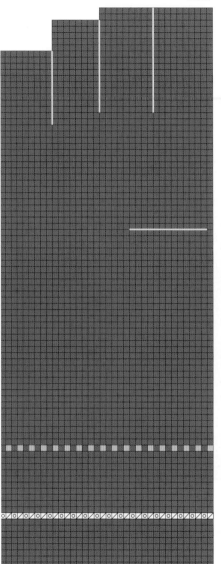

36 sts

RUST
GLOVES

Notes

Refer to Basic glove recipe for full instructions.

4 colours of yarn used: base colour (white), and 3 contrast colours (dark orange, dark brown and beige).

Instructions

1. Cast on 72 sts.

2. Divide equally between 4 needles on first round (18 sts per needle).

3. Work cuff following chart. Read chart from right to left and repeat twice.

4. Continue following chart with lace pattern on the 1st and 2nd needle for right hand glove and the 3rd and 4th needle for the left hand glove. Knit the stitches on the other two needles.

5. Continue following chart until the thumb position row.

6. Mark thumb with scrap yarn.

7. Continue following chart until you have reached the beginning of the little finger.

8. Work glove fingers with base colour.

9. Work thumb with base colour.

36 sts

WAVY
GLOVES

Notes

Refer to Basic glove recipe for full instructions.

3 colours of yarn used: base colour (white), and 2 contrast colours (navy and red).

Instructions

1. Cast on 72 sts.

2. Divide equally between 4 needles on first round (18 sts per needle).

3. Work cuff starting with Latvian Braid (see Cuff options) following charts. Read each chart from right to left.

4. Note that the front and back of glove each have a separate chart.

5. Continue following chart with lace pattern on the 1st and 2nd needle for right hand glove and the 3rd and 4th needle for the left hand glove. Knit the stitches on the other two needles.

6. Continue following charts until the thumb position row.

7. Mark thumb with scrap yarn.

8. Continue following charts until you have reached the beginning of the little finger.

9. Work glove fingers with base colour.

10. Work thumb with base colour.

Back

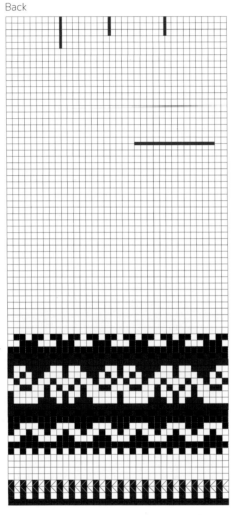

Front

Lat
Bra

36 sts

BLACK & WHITE
GLOVES

Notes

Refer to Basic glove recipe for full instructions.

2 colours of yarn used: base colour (black), and 1 contrast colour (white).

Instructions

1. Cast on 72 sts.

2. Divide equally between 4 needles on first round (18 sts per needle).

3. Work cuff following charts. Read each chart from right to left.

4. Continue with white pattern.

5. After white pattern knit 2 rounds with black yarn.

6. Continue following charts, with lace pattern on the 1st and 2nd needle for right hand glove and on the 3rd and 4th needle for the left hand glove. Knit the stitches on the other two needles.

7. Note that the front and back of glove each have a separate chart.

8. Continue following charts until the thumb position row.

9. Mark thumb with scrap yarn.

10. Continue following chart until you have reached the beginning of the little finger.

11. Work glove fingers with base colour.

12. Work thumb with base colour.

Back

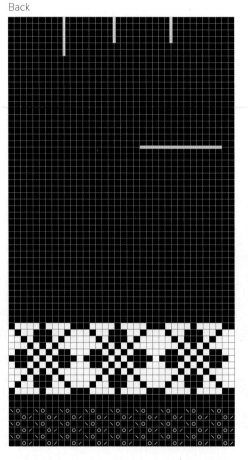

Front

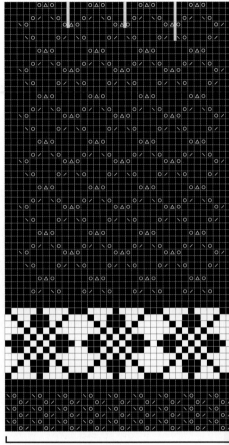

36 sts

ZIGZAG
GLOVES

Notes

Refer to Basic glove recipe for full instructions.

4 colours of yarn used: base colour (grey), and 3 contrast colours (navy, red and yellow).

Instructions

1. Cast on 72 sts.

2. Divide equally between 4 needles on first round (18 sts per needle).

3. Work cuff following charts. Read each chart from right to left.

4. Continue following charts until the thumb position row.

5. Note that the front and back of glove each have a separate chart.

6. Where indicated on chart, decrease by 1st with k2tog at the end of 2nd and 4th needle. 70 sts

7. Where indicated on chart, increase by 1st with M1 at the end of 2nd and 4th needle. 72 sts

8. Mark thumb with scrap yarn.

9. Continue following charts until you have reached the beginning of the little finger.

10. Work glove fingers with base colour.

11. Work thumb with base colour.

Back

Front

36 sts

JUMIS SIGN
GLOVES

Notes

Refer to Basic glove recipe for full instructions.

5 colours of yarn used: base colour (dark grey), and 4 contrast colours (white, red, green and yellow).

Instructions

1. Cast on 72 sts.

2. Divide equally between 4 needles on first round (18 sts per needle).

3. Work cuff following charts. Read each chart from right to left.

4. Note that the front and back of glove each have a separate chart.

5. Continue following charts until the thumb position row.

6. Mark thumb with scrap yarn.

7. Continue following charts until you have reached the beginning of the little finger.

8. Work glove fingers with base colour.

9. Work thumb with base colour.

Back

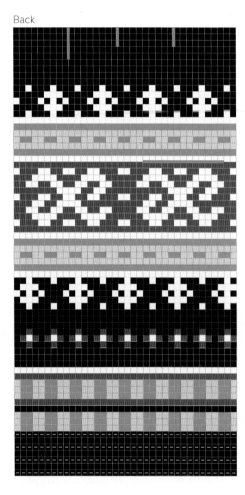

Front

36 sts

MARA'S CROSS
GLOVES

Notes

Refer to Basic glove recipe for full instructions.

6 colours of yarn used: base colour (black), and 5 contrast colours (white, navy, yellow, burgundy and red).

Instructions

1. Cast on 72 sts.

2. Divide equally between 4 needles on first round (18 sts per needle).

3. Work cuff following charts. Read each chart from right to left.

4. Note that the front and back of glove each have a separate chart.

5. Continue following charts until the thumb position row.

6. Mark thumb with scrap yarn.

7. Continue following charts until you have reached the beginning of the little finger.

8. Work glove fingers with base colour.

9. Work thumb with base colour.

Back

Front

36 sts

MORNING STAR
GLOVES

Notes

Refer to Basic glove recipe for full instructions.

6 colours of yarn used: base colour (light grey), and 5 contrast colours (dark grey, white, lilac, green and orange).

Instructions

1. Cast on 72 sts.

2. Divide equally between 4 needles on first round (18 sts per needle).

3. Work cuff following chart. Read chart from right to left and repeat twice.

4. Continue following chart until the thumb position row.

5. Mark thumb with scrap yarn.

6. Continue following chart until you have reached the beginning of the little finger.

7. Work glove fingers with base colour.

8. Work thumb with base colour.

36 sts

AUTUMN LEAVES
GLOVES

Notes

Refer to Basic glove recipe for full instructions.

4 colours of yarn used: base colour (navy), and 3 contrast colours (beige, yellow and orange).

Instructions

1. Cast on 72 sts.

2. Divide equally between 4 needles on first round (18 sts per needle).

3. Work cuff following charts. Read each chart from right to left.

4. Note that the front and back of glove each have a separate chart.

5. Continue following charts until the thumb position row.

6. Mark thumb with scrap yarn.

7. Continue following charts until you have reached the beginning of the little finger.

8. Work glove fingers with base colour.

9. Work thumb with base colour.

Back

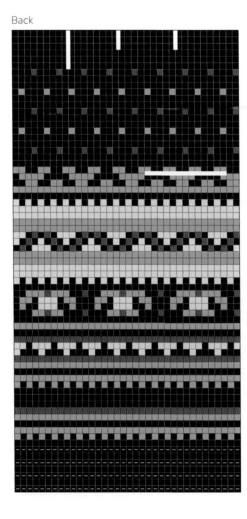

Front

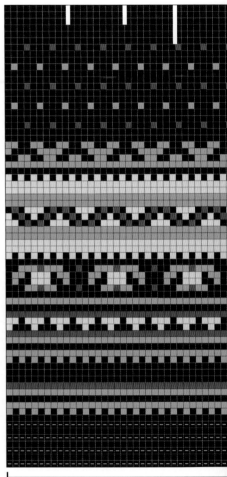

36 sts

SERPENT
GLOVES

Notes

Refer to Basic glove recipe for full instructions.

5 colours of yarn used: base colour (white), and 4 contrast colours (black, red, green and yellow).

Instructions

1. Cast on 72 sts.

2. Divide equally between 4 needles on first round (18 sts per needle).

3. Work cuff following charts. Read each chart from right to left.

4. Note that the front and back of glove each have a separate chart.

5. Continue following charts until the thumb position row.

6. Mark thumb with scrap yarn.

7. Continue following charts until you have reached the beginning of the little finger.

8. Work glove fingers with base colour.

9. Work thumb with base colour.

Back

Front

36 sts

LILAC
FINGERLESS GLOVES

Notes

Refer to Fingerless recipes for full instructions.

3 colours of yarn used: base colour (lilac), and 2 contrast colours (light pink and dark purple).

Instructions

1. Cast on 72 sts.

2. Divide equally between 4 needles on first round (18 sts per needle).

3. Work cuff starting with Latvian Braid (see Cuff options) following chart. Read chart from right to left and repeat twice.

4. Continue following chart until the thumb position row.

5. Mark thumb with scrap yarn.

6. Continue following chart until you reach the beginning of the little finger.

7. Work glove fingers with base colour.

8. Knit each finger until it reaches the upper joint of your finger, then cast off.

9. Work thumb with base colour, then cast off.

Latvian Braid

Latvian Braid

36 sts

PINK ROSE
FINGERLESS MITTENS

Notes

Refer to Fingerless recipes for full instructions.

4 colours of yarn used: base colour (light grey), and 3 contrast colours (pink, grey and white).

Instructions

1. Cast on 64 sts.

2. Divide equally between 4 needles on first round (16 sts per needle).

3. Work cuff following chart, working Latvian Braid (see Cuff options) where indicated. Read chart from right to left and repeat twice.

4. Continue following chart until the thumb position row.

5. Mark thumb over 16 sts between black lines.

6. Continue following chart until you have reached the upper joint of your little finger, then cast off all stitches.

7. Work thumb over 34 sts, repeating thumb chart twice and working each additional corner stitch in background colour at the end of each repeat.

8. When thumb chart is complete, cast off thumb sts.

Thumb

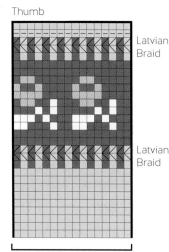

Latvian Braid

Latvian Braid

16 sts

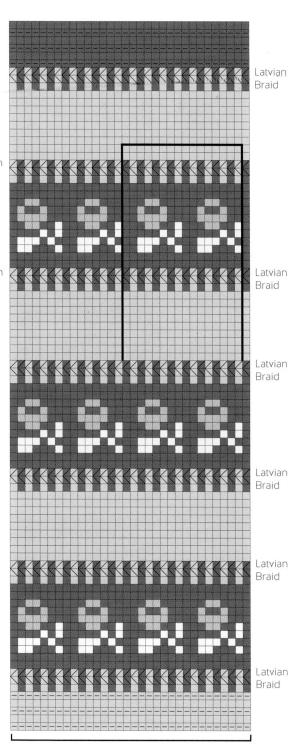

Latvian Braid

Latvian Braid

Latvian Braid

Latvian Braid

Latvian Braid

Latvian Braid

32 sts

BURGUNDY
FINGERLESS GLOVES

Notes

Refer to Fingerless recipes for full instructions.

2 colours of yarn used: base colour (burgundy), and 1 contrast colour (white).

Instructions

1. Cast on 72 sts.

2. Divide equally between 4 needles on first round (18 sts per needle).

3. Work cuff following chart. Read chart from right to left and repeat twice.

4. Continue following chart until the thumb position row.

5. Mark thumb with scrap yarn.

6. Continue following chart until you have reached the beginning of the little finger.

7. Work glove fingers with base colour.

8. Knit each finger until it reaches the upper joint of your finger, then cast off.

9. Work thumb with base colour, then cast off.

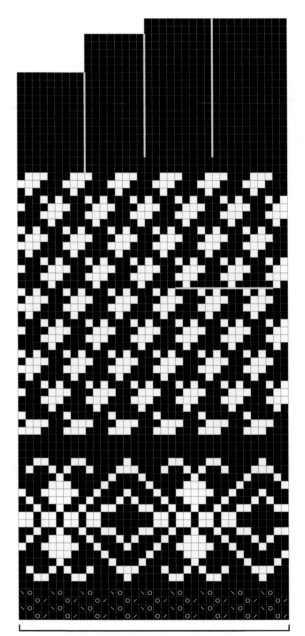

36 sts

WHITE BRAID
GLOVES

Notes

Refer to Basic glove recipe for full instructions.

1 colour of yarn used: white.

Instructions

1. Cast on 72 sts.

2. Divide equally between 4 needles on first round (18 sts per needle).

3. Work cuff following charts. Read each chart from right to left.

4. Note that the front and back of glove each have a separate chart.

5. Continue following charts, with lace pattern on the 1st and 2nd needle for right hand glove and the 3rd and 4th needle for left hand glove. Knit the stitches on the other two needles.

6. Continue following charts until the thumb position row.

7. Mark thumb with scrap yarn.

8. Continue following charts until you have reached the beginning of the little finger.

9. Work glove fingers.

10. Work thumb.

Back

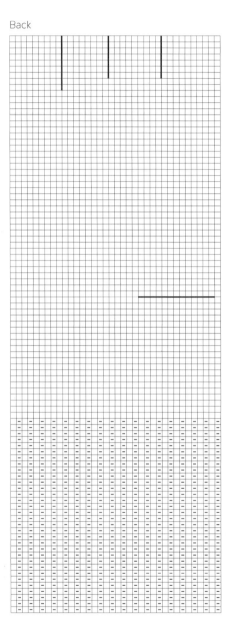

Front

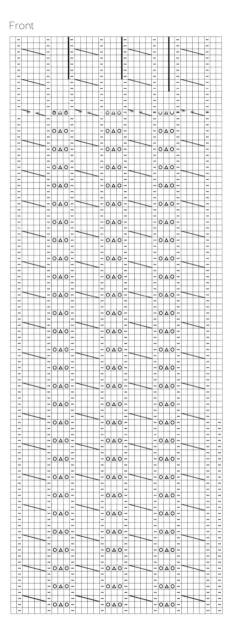

36 sts

ABOUT THE AUTHOR

Ieva Ozolina is the founder and creator of the Hobbywool and the "Knit Like a Latvian" kits. Ieva started knitting when she was 14 and has been passionate about knitting ever since. In 2009 she started her own knitting and yarn company called "Hobbywool".

Ieva has taken her "Knit Like a Latvian" knitting kits to over 40 international fairs and exhibitions to spread her love for Latvian mittens all over the world. Her books have been translated into 14 languages.

Ieva lives in Riga, Latvia, and runs her yarn shop in the Old Town of Riga together with her husband Maris.

THANK YOU

First of all I want to thank all Latvian women, who have knitted mittens for centuries, keeping traditions alive and leaving us with the most robust and beautiful heritage of mitten patterns.

I want to thank Sarah Callard, Commissioning Editor at David and Charles, who offered me the great opportunity to write this book.

A special thanks to Janis Pitens, who made the pattern chart drawings and has been my biggest help in creating this book.

Thanks to Dr.hist Aija Jansone, whose books and wide knowledge about Latvian mittens and knitting traditions inspired me to create my own "Knit Like a Latvian" mitten knitting kits as well as to write this book.

Thanks to Lubov Yakimova and Dina Gravite for help with all the knitting.

Thanks to Hobbywool team member Iveta Kulina for all the help throughout the creation of this book.

And last but not least a BIG thanks to my dear family for all the support.

SUPPLIERS

Hobbywool 2-ply 100% wool yarns are made in Latvia and are the perfect choice for colourwork knitting and especially mittens. All yarns are made only from natural fibres and at Hobbywool you will find a wide range of colours – from earth tones to bright colours.

All Hobbywool yarns and knitting tools can be purchased direct from:

www.hobbywool.com

Index

A DAVID AND CHARLES BOOK
© David and Charles Ltd 2024

David and Charles is an imprint of David and Charles, Ltd
Suite A, Tourism House, Pynes Hill, Exeter, EX2 5WS

Text and Designs © Ieva Ozolina 2024
Layout and Photography © David and Charles, Ltd 2024

First published in the UK and USA in 2024

Some of the content in this book was previously published in Knit Like a Latvian (2018) and Knit Like a Latvian: Accessories (2021).

ISBN-13: 9781446312667 paperback
ISBN-13: 9781446312674 EPUB
ISBN-13: 9781446312681 PDF

This book has been printed on paper from approved suppliers and made from pulp from sustainable sources.

Printed in China through Asia Pacific Offset for:
David and Charles, Ltd
Suite A, Tourism House, Pynes Hill, Exeter, EX2 5WS

Publishing Director: Ame Verso
Senior Comissioing Editor: Sarah Callard
Managing Editor: Jeni Chown
Editor: Jessica Cropper
Project Editor: Tricia Gilbert
Head of Design: Anna Wade
Designer: Blanche Williams
Pre-press Designer: Susan Reansbury
Illustrations: Kuo Kang Chen
Art Direction: Sarah Rowntree
Photography: Jason Jenkins
Production Manager: Beverley Richardson

David and Charles publishes high-quality books on a wide range of subjects. For more information visit www.davidandcharles.com.

Share your makes with us on social media using #dandcbooks and follow us on Facebook and Instagram by searching for @dandcbooks.

Layout of the digital edition of this book may vary depending on reader hardware and display settings.